PRAISE FOR *DEEP WATER*

Jonathan Lewis' very transparent account of his struggles with fatherlessness comes from deep personal experience. His Christian journey, wise counsel, and the strong example that I know him to be today should be a great encouragement to anyone who is dealing with this in their own life. Anyone who has experienced fatherlessness should be encouraged by Jonathan Lewis' account of his personal Christian journey through the depth of despair to a life that today serves as a great example of how God's grace can transform a person.

Jacques Lapointe
CEO, GlaxoSmithKline Europe, retired
Chair of the Board, Teen Challenge Canada

Embracing and sharing our story can be hard but Jonathan steps up and owns his story and shares it wonderfully. He bravely explores his own life, vulnerabilities, and he comes from a place of love so that we may benefit from his journey and discover our own place and impact. Given our world today, thank you Jonathan for sharing.

Wayne Crawley
Partner, Venor

If you are a man who senses that you have more of your best to bring to the world, read this book and be ready for the transformation Jonathan Lewis has laid out for us to grow through. Not only does he shine the light on a deep and pervasive issue facing our world, he lays out a clear framework to overcoming it and achieving deeper fulfillment in your life. If you open your heart, and are willing to go deep, you will surely emerge a better man to serve those in your life at a higher level.

Manley Feinberg, II
World Class Climber and Motivational Speaker
Author of "Reaching Your Next Summit!"

Jonathan's book is so powerfully written to encourage all fathers and men on any level! It's as if he has his arm around you and is looking you right in the eye with the hard truth and biggest heart. He makes it personal, but in the very best way, igniting action that is grounded in the psychology and the spirit of necessary change that can transcend your biggest challenges. He draws out the courage within to address the deepest challenges and mentors you to rise to being the man you will be so proud to be.

Laura Sontrop
Psychotherapist, MA Clinical Psychology

For anyone who has lost a loved one, this book will show that you are not alone. Jonathan takes us on a journey of compassion, loss, and redemption—to a better place. A book that will resonate with readers of all ages.

Irene E. Pfeiffer, C.M.
President, Moorgate Holdings and Order of Canada

Jonathan Lewis is so compassionate in all he does. His insight and investment in his friends, co-workers, and clients is authentic and heart-felt. He inspires so many people in so many ways. Hard work is visible in his day-to-day life and is reflective as a testament to the commitment he brings to everything he does. I'm proud to call him a friend, and I'm thankful for his financial counsel for my family for these past twenty years. Jesus be with you forever, amen and God Bless.

Peter Lawen
VP Property Management, Paramount Management

Jonathan's passion for impacting change is both personal and profound. His courage and openness in sharing his own story is sure to resonate with many other dads who may be struggling.

Starr Cunningham
CEO, Mental Health Foundation for NS

Jonathan's honesty and vulnerability is refreshing and challenging. His important message, which comes from a place of experience, is one that needs to be heard! Jonathan tells his story in a way that hits home for many people, myself included! Fatherlessness is a problem in our society that more people need to talk about. Jonathan's story has challenged me to consider where my self-worth comes from. It's provoked me to look to my Heavenly Father for leadership, and to step up to the plate as a man!

Spenser Mason
Development Officer, Teen Challenge Atlantic

Jonathan poignantly describes from his life experience the profound impact of a father in the life of his child and the source of hope for those who have lost that cornerstone in their life.

Mark DeJager
Missionary and Pastor

Deep Water

Jonathan Lewis

Deep Water

Jonathan Lewis

How to Face Fatherlessness, Fill the Gap, and Be the Man God Made You to Be.

Paperback ISBN: 978-1-945255-86-1
Ebook ISBN: 978-1-945255-87-8

Printed in the United States of America.

Cover Design: Tim Murray
Layout Design: Dagne Ode
Lead Writer: Angela Tewalt
Editor: Cameron Brooks
Proofing Editor and Publishing Manager: Amy Rollinger

Throne Publishing Group
2329 N Career Ave #215
Sioux Falls, SD 57107
ThronePG.com

TABLE OF CONTENTS

DEDICATION

To my precious daughters Maddy and Clara and my beautiful wife, Sara.
These breadcrumbs are for you.

INTRODUCTION

Years ago, I was barely holding on. I was disengaged, in denial, and a novice on manhood. I was defensive and irresponsible, and I was missing my dad. I thought that without him, I would never have the guidance and encouragement I needed to be a strong man.

But I was wrong.

I give you this story because I was fatherless, too. I know that fatherlessness is real, visceral, and stifling if a heart is left broken. But I also know that "God uses broken and imperfect people to challenge and inspire others. He utilizes our mistakes, our brokenness, and our victories to shine a light on the path so that others might follow" (*The Hole in our Gospel* by Richard Stearns, president of World Vision). So here I am, extending my hand with all my might and encouraging you to get real with God and live out your authentic self.

Don't settle. Don't be content to be mediocre or ineffective. Push for something transcendent—something that goes beyond simply building your castle and living in it. You owe yourself more! It's time to live with the understanding that there is a God who wants to be our Father, and if we are willing, He will show us the way. Luke 11:9 says, "ask, and it will be given to you; seek, and you will find; knock and it will be opened to you."

Today, I know my Father. 2 Corinthians 6:18 says, "I will be a father to you, and you shall be sons and daughters to me, says the Lord Almighty." I know I have a brother in Jesus Christ who is showing me my Father's ways.

I think God wants every man to take up this challenge with Him as our guide. It takes a real man to step into the ring of life with faith in God as his only source of strength and get his hands dirty. We were meant for something more! Today, I know my Father, I am on fire for Christ, and I am ready to show you the way when you are.

"Thus says the LORD: 'stand by the roads, and look, and ask for the ancient paths, where the good way is, and walk in it, and find rest for your souls,' " Jeremiah 6:16.

Part One
The Void

chapter one:

Becoming Fatherless

Becoming Fatherless

When I was a young boy, I loved September. And it wasn't because the leaves were changing colour or because of the crisp smells in the air. It was because the first Monday of October was near, and the first Monday of October was the opening of bird hunting season in Nova Scotia.

On that day, I knew my dad and I would take off from school and work, and we would be up at four in the morning, in the truck and heading to the woods. We'd have our sandwiches and our soup, and we would spend fourteen hours together, in the apple orchards and surrounding woods walking around looking for our quarry, having lunch together and shooting a partridge or a pheasant if we saw one. In the traditional sense, I would be learning from Dad during this time, and I would be learning the basics of manhood. We were father and son, in nature, hunting for our supper for that weekend, and *I loved it.*

That thrill carried into deer season and then into rabbit season and even into Christmas, Dad's favourite holiday. October through December was the best time of year for me because I got to spend time with my dad.

When I was growing up, I didn't care how nice of a house we had, how nice of a car we had, how much money we spent, or even how often we went on vacation. What I cared about most was spending time with my dad. He was a busy, working man who had a deep desire to make his mark, provide for his family, and feel valuable in the world, and that made it difficult to get in time with him. So I coveted it.

I coveted every bit of time I could get with my dad, and I miss him every single day.

His name was Wayne Lewis, and he was bigger than life. He captured people's attention in a gregarious way, and he had a vibrant personality. He was light-hearted, too, and he knew how to have fun. He could shift gears from "work mode" to "fun mode" better than anyone I've ever known. And when he was with you, you knew you had his attention 100 percent!

My dad was a hard-working businessman with great integrity. I saw him suffer in business because he wouldn't follow other men in their weaknesses. Instead, he did whatever was right, and he was extremely generous. He was fearless, too. He was never limited by fear but instead faced it head-on. I think it was a tremendous demonstration of his masculinity. Not in a beat-your-chest kind of way, but in a personally triumphant kind of way, saying, "This is what I am trying to achieve. Fear will not stop me." He demonstrated that all the time, and it never did.

Most of all, my dad was committed to his family. He loved us all very much, and that's important to say, because he didn't have that kind of loving upbringing. My grandfather was a WWII vet. He fought with the Canadian infantry throughout the Italian and European theaters of war with the British forces, and he saw some horrific events that led him to suffer PTSD. As a result, my dad grew up in an abusive home. Like many men who came back from that war, my grandfather didn't know how to deal with it, so he turned to alcohol, and alcohol turned into violence in the home and, being the oldest brother of three, my dad got the worst of it.

Even still, my dad was forgiving, and I realize now that was a deliberate choice. It was also a demonstration of real character. He was deliberate about loving his father and recognizing that his father was damaged and that wasn't necessarily who his father really was. So he loved him anyhow.

Then, when my dad had a family of his own, he wanted to break that cycle of abuse, and he did—with mixed results. There was physical abuse in my home growing up. When my dad was under a lot of stress, I learned to stay clear of him. I can remember my uncle saying they had a "sneakers on" rule growing up because they never knew when "the old man" would come home drunk. I adopted the same "sneakers on" rule of thumb with my dad when he was under the gun. The physical abuse was limited—I can count on one hand the number of times I experienced hard, physical abuse—and it was only me, never toward my sisters. On the contrary, they grew up very different. My dad really poured into them, nurtured and loved them completely, and I think growing up with a mother who was abused was the reason for that.

For me, it was more verbal abuse, but I know my dad simply wanted to live vicariously through his son and see me do more than he ever had the opportunity to do. So he was tough on me, but I still always felt loved. He used to give me a light backhand and say, "That's for nothing. Wait until you do something." It was his way of saying, "I love you." He never said "I love you" to me, but he had his own way of demonstrating it. And I knew he did.

Seeking God

In the months and years leading up to my dad's death, God's Holy Spirit really started to work in him, I believe. He hadn't gone to church with us as a family in years, because he had become very hardened against the church. He would say that people in the church hurt him or that people in the church in business took advantage of him, so he was out. This was not in line with my dad's forgiving nature. But toward the end of his life, he came back around, nearly full circle, and it was like the Holy Spirit revealed to him that he had a responsibility to his family to lead us spiritually, and so he really started making the effort. He started attending church with us again and talking about God and his desire to acknowledge Him in our family and lives.

Even further, he was making his rounds and catching up with his oldest, longest friends, as if he had this revelation that his time was growing short. Our whole family agrees today that it was like *he knew*. For a man who grew up in the '50s and '60s, and who's favourite movies mirrored Clint Eastwood Westerns, and just that '70s version of what manhood was supposed to be, my dad suddenly *changed*. Instead of *The Good, The Bad, and The Ugly,* one of his favourite Eastwood Westerns, he was tender, engaged, and loving.

He became soft. He was crying, and I'd never seen my dad cry! He was telling Mom that he loved her—and that's not to say he never did. Even though he was hard on me, he was really good to her and taught me how to love a woman. But he was pouring into her even more and demonstrating his love for all of us in bigger ways than he ever had before.

Twelve days before my dad died, I walked into his office early one morning, and he was sitting there in his underwear. I was always up early because I had a lot of jobs. Dad always taught us a strong work ethic, so I was delivering papers, pumping gas, you name it. But anyway, that morning, I was up early to work before school, and I noticed my dad was sitting in his office in his underwear, crying. He turned to me, in tears, and said, "Jonathan, I love you."

Now, when you are a fifteen-year-old boy and you have a dad who never tells you something like that, you don't really know how to respond! I did say, "I love you, too, Dad," but I remember thinking to myself, "But I'm not going to hug you, because you are in your underwear, and this is getting weird!" I think I sort of high-fived him, and that was it, but it's a scene I'll never forget.

Then, the week before he died, it was Father's Day. It was a Sunday and we were at church as a family. Our Pastor Russell Knowles preached a sermon about fatherhood and our responsibilities as men. Pastor Knowles, true to form, delivered a call to action to men, and my dad responded to the call. He came up to Pastor Knowles right then and told him that he felt he really had failed us as a father and that he wanted to step up. He wanted to be there for us. This was uncharacteristic of my dad. Looking back, I realize that call to manhood was for me today as much as it was for any of the fathers in that room then.

Seven days later, my dad drowned.

The Day I Lost my Dad

Baseball was a very big deal in our family. Aside from bird hunting, the other time I coveted most with my dad was on the diamond, especially when he was coaching me or hitting fly balls to me. It was wonderful to be with him. He would heckle me from home plate and tell me what I was doing wrong. Whenever I made a good snag of a ball, I would get that unceremonious grunt from the plate that made my heart soar because I knew he was impressed with my hustle. It wasn't an accolade, but it put fuel in my tank.

On this June weekend in 1991, we both had double-headers. My dad was playing men's competitive intermediate fast-pitch, and I was playing competitive rep ball for Team Nova Scotia out of Halifax. We had been one of the top teams in the country the year previous! But Dad made the executive decision not to play baseball that weekend and to instead spend time as a family. So we did.

That Saturday, he rented scuba gear and tanks, and on Sunday we went out to a beautiful spot we knew well called Sandy Cove. It's a smaller, lesser-known lighthouse that is the quintessential Nova Scotia. It's the most beautiful, little horse shoe-shaped cove out of granite rock, with white sandy beaches and thirty-five feet of perfectly crystal clear north Atlantic water.

Now, Nova Scotia is nicknamed the Graveyard of the Atlantic because of its treacherous surrounding waters and numerous shipwrecks. The area has a lot of shoals and frequent rough seas, and nearby Sable Island is always shifting and therefore has very rough waters and thick fog. The shipwrecks are so many that if you blacked out an entire map of Nova Scotia then lit up all the wrecks, you could still see the entire map of it. Wrecks outline the entire province.

Moreover, where we were diving in Sandy Cove has several known shipwrecks, including the SS Atlantic, a transatlantic ocean liner of the White Star Line that operated between Liverpool, UK, and New York City in 1873. During its voyage, the ship ran into rocks and sank, killing over 500 people and remaining the deadliest civilian maritime disaster in the North Atlantic Ocean until the loss of Titanic in 1912.

Yes, we knew of the treacherous waters, but we had visited there many times as a family, and we enjoyed it. I was only fifteen years old, so I wasn't a certified diver yet, but I knew my way around dive gear pretty well. It was supposed to be a fun weekend of family time together.

That morning, my mom and dad went diving together and had a great time, but my mom didn't want to do the second dive, even though we had the air for it. So that afternoon, just Dad and I went out while my mom and younger sister watched from ashore. And I didn't dive with my dad. I put on weight belts with my wetsuit, and I just went free-diving with him.

We were spearfishing flounder, and I was carrying the catch bag. He would go along the bottom and spear the flounder while I followed along the surface. We were anywhere from ten to thirty feet deep. But with my weights, I had no problem getting down and up.

We had caught several nice flounder and my Dad was following a big one. An Atlantic wolffish—an ugly dog fish that eats flounder—was following the flounder, too. So the wolffish was following the flounder, and dad was following both of them, getting ready to steal that wolffish's supper. But suddenly, Dad started to ascend.

It was a controlled ascent, a technique used in scuba diving when you come up slower than your bubbles and you exhale as you come. This ensures your lungs don't burst like a balloon from the expanding air in your lungs as the pressure on your body lowers when you approach the surface. Even though his ascent was unexpected, I had absolutely no reason to think there was anything wrong. My only thought was, "Why did you let that flounder go?!"

When he got to the surface, I could only see him intermittently. Even on a calm day and in a shallow cove in the North Atlantic, there are significant swells. So when Dad came to the surface, I went over a swell and couldn't see him, then I went down a swell and he came up over the next one. It all happens very quickly, but you can't exactly sit on the surface and have a chat unless you are holding onto one another.

I finally swam to him, and because my dad was always such a clown and always carrying on, I didn't think anything of it when he started to grab at me and pull at my mask. I hate to say it, but my response was, "What are you doing, you asshole!" But he kept up, and he wasn't saying anything. That's when I knew something was wrong.

He grabbed at me again, and now there was gear

at the surface. He had a glove off, our catch bag was floating, our spears were floating, and his mask was off. I realized my dad was in trouble. I never once in my life thought of my dad as anything but strong, deliberate, reliable, disciplined, bigger than life, and fearless, but what I saw in my father's eyes at that moment was a completely terrified and petrified man. In his eyes was pure panic. I will never forget it.

Because I was not properly trained as a diver, I did not know then what I so obviously know now, having dove now for many, many years, which is to drop his weight belt and fill his BCD, which would have left him floating like a fishing bobber on the surface. Instead, I was now gripped with the same panic. Because he was flailing at the surface, I did what I think any young kid would do, and I dove underneath him. I swam up between his legs and tried to hold him up so he could sort out whatever was wrong. I was assuming there was an issue with his gear or that he got a mouthful of water and just needed to collect himself. But that effort only seemed to accomplish one thing: I utterly exhausted myself.

After a lot of fatigue, I came up and was trying to hold onto him, but another swell came, and I lost him. After I got my mask on, I looked for him again and found him about ten feet below me, floating face down and sinking. So I dove.

I grabbed him and pulled him back to the surface, but at this point, he was no longer moving. He was just so heavy and I was being pulled down with him. I managed to get back to the surface for air and started to holler for help. My mom and sister were on the shore—I can't even imagine what my mom was going through. But she didn't have a wetsuit, and if she were to jump in and try to help, she would have likely died herself of hypothermia or from the life-and-death struggle that was taking place. It was up to me.

There were two divers who had just gone into shore, and I could see them on the beach. They wouldn't have had a lot of air left in their tanks because they had just finished their dives, but they started to put their gear back on to come help me. There also was a fisherman who lived close by who heard me in the water, so he ran out to his dory to come help. And while they made their way to me, I marked my dad by staying on top of him, fighting the currents on the surface while the undercurrents were dragging him deeper. Of course, I made several more dives down to try and bring him up, but at that point, he was nearly twenty feet under, like a starfish face down with no bubbles coming up. He was not breathing. He was not moving.

The guy with the dory got to me first. I asked what he had for gear. He had some shark fishing line, a large shark hook, and an anchor. So I told him to gear up the shark hook and the line. It was strong enough to do what I had in mind. It was very tidal at the time, so I knew I had to get out ahead of Dad with the shark hook, drag the hook along the bottom and let the tide carry it until it hit his body and then hook into some part of his gear, his 8-mm wetsuit or his flesh, then start pulling up. But I was so tired, it was all I had left in me to do. Even on the surface, water kept spilling into my snorkel as his weight pulled me down while the dory hit my head several times.

I started pulling and got him to about ten feet from the surface at one point. I realize now that I should have just tried to bring him all the way to the surface since I clearly had him this time, but I was afraid the hook would rip free again and I'd lose him, so just as I gave the line to the fella in the dory, Dad broke away from me. I dove frantically to catch him before he sank again, this time kicking for everything I was worth, but I was drifting.

When you let go of someone who is your whole world—how do you come back from that?

I had no strength left, and I could not get him to the surface. My lungs were full of water, and I was almost drowning myself. So I let him go.

When you let go of someone who is your whole world—how do you come back from that?

As I let him go, his body rolled over onto his back, and there was no life in his eyes. His eyes were open, but he was gone, and it was like I had failed him. He just sank, away from me and into the cold, dark blue water, as I watched him disappear.

Facing Fatherlessness

Once the divers made it out, one of the guys dove down with the little bit of air he had left, brought Dad up, and we got him into the dory. It had been maybe seven or eight minutes at this point, but we got him onto shore and one of the divers started giving him CPR. They were trying to take his gear off and loosen up his wetsuit. I was lying flat on the beach next to him. I had no strength left.

When I had let go of Dad during that final attempt in the water, the sky had clouded over, ominously. It had been an otherwise beautiful day, but in that last glance of Dad sinking down, there was a darkness to the sky that amplified his disappearance into the blue. But then, as we had him on shore, the sun returned, and it was a beautiful, sunny day again. Beautiful and perfect, yet our lives had instantly changed forever.

The police and paramedics arrived. They worked on Dad on the beach, then all the way into the city in the ambulance ahead of us, which was about a 30-minute drive to the hospital. I just remember sitting in the waiting room with my mom and sister just praying. Just praying. Just praying, "Please God, don't let this be so."

I kept thinking, "This can't be happening. How can this be happening right now?" But as the doctor came to us, he looked at my mom, looked at my younger sister, Jennifer, then to me and said, "I'm sorry. The paramedics could not revive him. He is gone."

I wanted to see him. The only memory I had of my dad at that point was letting him go in the water. My mom didn't want me to, but I insisted. I needed to see my dad. When I went in, he was blue and lifeless. You could tell they had worked on him a ton. But it was just Dad and me. There was no one else in the room, so I laid across his cold lifeless body, and I pleaded, "God, nothing is beyond you. Don't take my dad. Please, don't take my dad!"

But he was gone, and I suddenly became fatherless.

I'm a grown man now, and to this day, I don't know why my dad drowned. He made a controlled ascent, which gave no indication of emergency. The fact that I never figured out what happened is why I was hurting for so many years. Today, I have peace in my heart, beautiful children and my own family to provide for, but I don't have my dad. When I think about him, it's like an unfinished work. He knew what he had to do, and even though he struggled to do it, he set the tone. He let me know in more ways than one how to live a life of purpose, and how

He let me know in more ways than one how to live a life of purpose, and how to complete the task.

to complete the task. So that's what I'm doing. I am facing my fatherlessness, and now you can, too.

chapter two:

What is Fatherlessness?

What is Fatherlessness?

The next day was a Monday, and I tried to open my Bible, just searching for some kind of comfort. It's like I needed some sort of explanation from God. I opened to the center of the Bible and happened upon Lamentations 3:31-33, "For the Lord will not cast off forever, but, though he cause grief, he will have compassion according to the abundance of his steadfast love; for he does not afflict from his heart or grieve the children of men."

It was like God was answering my prayer, trying to plead with me, "I don't know how to make you understand this, Jonathan, but I do not want you to suffer, and I love you!" I wish I could say I embraced that with an open and trusting heart, but instead, I struggled. For the next four or five years as a teenager, I was anything but a triumphant believer.

And so grief set in.

The funeral was such a tragedy. My dad was so well-liked and had a lot of Christian and non-Christian friends, baseball buddies and all his workmates and family there, but when you attend the funeral of a young man who dies in an unexpected accident and then leaves his young family behind, the entire congregation is shocked. We were just playing baseball and sharing jokes four days ago! And then he was gone.

Pastor Knowles presided over the funeral, and he in no uncertain terms shared the story of Jesus' life and His love for each of us. People were really impacted, and I was proud of Pastor Knowles for having the courage to share how God loves us and how dying is a part of this life. He drove home that it is what we do and who we do it for while we are here that counts. To this day, I know seeds were planted and lives were impacted at Dad's funeral. Even in his death, how he lived still echoes in the lives of people he knew.

Even in his death, how he lived still echoes in the lives of people he knew.

He continues to inspire my life every day.

After the funeral, the world moved on, yet we were left feeling like our world had completely shattered. It was the beginning of summer—such an exciting time for a kid!—but our usual routine didn't even exist, and it was one of the worst summers of my life. We were all in denial. My mom was completely numb—as if she wasn't even there—but she was thrust back into the workplace trying to make sense of Dad's businesses, and it was all too much.

And I felt so, so alone. There is never an easy way to lose a parent, especially in those formative years. But not only did I lose a parent, I lost my dad who was bigger than life. I also had to deal with the trauma and the guilt that I somehow failed him. There was no way I could have prepared for the long road ahead of me.

Fatherlessness is the Absence of Leadership

It was easy to see during this time that I was my father's son, because I was really getting angry at how life was going. Without my dad, I felt as though I had no guide in life anymore. There was no one to break trail for me—be it the right trail or the wrong one, there was simply no point of reference from which to even begin. My dad was my leader in the jungle of life, and then he was gone. I couldn't even make one last call to him for some kind of parting wisdom. There was no map, no compass, no trail, just his hat there on the floor of the jungle of life that I, as his only son, had to pick up and put

Without my dad, I felt as though I had no guide in life anymore. There was no one to break trail for me.

on to guide my life on my own. But which way do I go? For a season, I just sat there.

Most men tend to live out a false self. But I didn't even have time to be false; I had to simply survive. I had to grow up in a hurry! There was a real, present wound at play, and with that wound came this message of, "You are on your own now, and no one cares. This is your fault." With my dad by my side, I had direction, I had confidence, I had a foundation, and I had a safety net. We all ache to have a father who says, "I'm proud of you. I love you, and I am right here for you. Your mom and I are here for you, so don't be scared to jump, because if you fall, we will catch you!" I was wounded, in a fight for my life, and the wound was my safety net removed before I was ready, and I was not equipped for the free fall below.

We all ache to have a father who says, "I'm proud of you. I love you, and I am right here for you."

In his book *Wild at Heart*, John Eldredge addresses the origins of masculinity. He writes, "The plan from the beginning of time was that a father would lay the foundation for a young boy's heart and pass on to him that essential knowledge and confidence in his strength. A father would be the first man in a boy's life, and forever the most important. Above all, he would answer *the* question for his son, 'Do I have what it takes?' and give him his name."

How powerful! I think this is true for all children, that we need a father to encourage us and believe in us and to whom we can depend on. Even Jesus needed that affirmation. After Jesus is baptized, God says from heaven, "You are my beloved Son; with you I am well pleased" (Luke 3:22). I think He is saying here, "Jesus, you have what it takes! You can do this!" We, too, need this from our earthly fathers, a vote of confidence, a father to trust. We need that intimate refuge where we go when the going is really, really tough. Jesus later demonstrates this in Gethsemane on the Mount of Olives just before he is arrested and crucified, when he is praying, "Father, if you are willing, remove this cup from me. Nevertheless, not my will, but yours, be done" (22:42).

'Do I have what it takes?'

Jesus knows what is before him. He is about to die for the sins of all humanity. So what does He do? He goes to his dad, who sends an angel from heaven, and the angel *strengthens* him. To me, that so eloquently demonstrates the bond of father and son in the face of adversity. A father's leadership gave the son power.

My dad was my leader, and I believe that fatherlessness is the absence of leadership. It is no longer having that protector, provider, nurturer, mentor and safety net below our fears. And when leadership is no longer near, feelings of inadequacy take root, and a son falls prey to an impoverished spirit. Heartbreak, loneliness, and disappointment lead to a marred identity dictated only by the world, and these broken spirits suddenly don't see themselves as empowered and strong as they did under their father's wing. They instead see themselves as failed children, as I did, and they resign any hope in themselves or their potential.

George MacDonald captures our struggle with lost identity well when he says, "The hardest, gladdest thing in the world is to *cry Father!* from a full heart—the refusal to look up to God as our father is the one central misery" (*Abba, Father* by George MacDonald). *The one central misery.* That's worth thinking about. Fatherlessness has become so normal that we don't see the depth of the void and the damage it is creating in our homes, communities, and society.

Fatherlessness has become so normal that we don't see the depth of the void and the damage it is creating in our homes, communities, and society.

In fatherlessness, there is a lack of confidence, a need for affirmation, and a sudden deferring to others for strength. Pride may take over, or a need to compensate by being an adrenaline junkie or striving for financial success, as was the case with me.

Some men may wander, becoming globetrotters

who never stop searching for the next hidden oasis to heal themselves, but to no avail. Every man has an explorer in him, but these wanderers seek the unknown driven by fear on an unhealthy path. Or, they may check out altogether, filling their lives with self-destructive behavior or useless pastimes like video games, unhealthy sexual encounters, drugs, drinking, or hanging out with other emotionally-stunted men. None of this leads to affirmation or confidence. It only leads to increased loneliness and fear, and I have seen it over and over—false bravado to keep them safe.

The thoughts and actions I succumbed to were the opposite of a positive mindset. Instead of feeling full, I felt hopeless. Instead of being able to breathe into others' lives, I had at best money to offer to soothe my need for purpose. I wanted to quit, I told myself I was no good, and I lamented on how lonely I was. I felt fear as my constant nemesis and companion, and fear is predicated on worry and doubt. Poet David Whyte says, "The price of our vitality is the sum of all our fears." So many men live out of fear! But the question is, *Why?* On top of hopelessness and self-loathing, I also felt jealous around other fathers and sons, wishing I had my dad back to show me the way. Because without him, I had no sense of direction. And when we lose our way, it's easy to wander.

Self-Worth

There are two types of fatherlessness. One is physical fatherlessness, which is the absence of him. I experienced a traumatic event, and I in no uncertain terms lost my father. He was once in my life in a grandiose way, and now he is absent. The other is emotional fatherlessness, which is a subtler lack of an emotional connection and engagement with an otherwise physically present father figure. Some might not even know they are experiencing emotional fatherlessness.

Some men may grow up in an environment where even though a father is present, there is no leadership, no empowerment, and no one to say, "You are a superstar! I believe in you!" And if you didn't grow up with that, how do you even know there is an alternative way? How do you even know how beautiful it should be?

Emotional fatherlessness creates a tendency to push away from healthy relationships and a continued insecurity in oneself. And both physical and emotional fatherlessness promote low self-worth, which also brings about unhealthy relationships.

I truly believe that all children define their self-worth based not only on the presence of a father but by the love he did or did not give them. For young men, a father teaches them things only a man can, such as how to love and respect a woman and how to sacrifice for those he loves. And a father helps a man answer the biggest question of all, "Dad, do I have what it takes?"

Although I coveted the time I spent with my dad, my relationship with him really hurt my self-worth. I know it was an unfinished work for him, but as an adult today, I have to constantly reaffirm my worth. I need to go to scripture and trust my Heavenly Father when He affirms his value in me. "For God so loved the world, that he gave his only Son" (John 3:16). Or, put another way, "Jonathan, for God so loved *you* that He gave His only Son so you, too, could have sonship with Him." People who have good relationships with their dads can say, "Oh, yeah, that resonates with me, because I saw that in my earthly parents." But for someone who is experiencing physical or emotional fatherlessness, there is a void, and it's therefore more difficult to accept those words. You don't trust the truth in it.

You need a father, a constant leader, and someone whose promises you can hang your hat on. I think that is found in God.

The Fatherless Have an Advantage

For a long time, I believed that my father's absence put me at such a disadvantage in life. I kept thinking that with him by my side, only then could I have leadership, foundation, and direction. Today, I realize that even though I miss my dad every day, I'm actually at an *advantage*, because I have no choice *but* to trust in God. In the face of adversity, if I want guidance, I get to turn to God and grow *even deep-*

er in relationship with Him than perhaps I would if I had an earthly present father to rely on instead. And so I have. I have turned to my Heavenly Father—and here's the thing, there is no safety net. A relationship with God is a powerful connection between you and your Heavenly Father. And it is enough. If you have preconceptions about God and His love for you, I challenge you in your thinking. You, too, can turn to a Heavenly Father and be in relationship with Him. *You can.*

We all have an ache for the perfect father. But as we watch our earthly fathers grow and mature, we start to recognize their flaws. Just like my dad saw the flaws in his father and I saw flaws in mine, we merely reconcile and accept them for who they are and know they did the best they could. But what also transpires in that reconciliation is still a hunger for our one and only perfect Father in our perfect Savior. Augustine says, "Thou hast formed us for Thyself, and our hearts are restless till they find their rest in Thee" (Augustine, *Confessions—Book 1*).

I had a friend tell me once, "I know you love the Lord and have a deep heart to serve Him, but, Jonathan, you can just rest in him, too. You don't have to do the work. You don't have to earn his love or prove anything to anyone. You still are clinging to your old nature, your default position, which is to strive, but God doesn't want you to do that. *You are not inadequate.* You are valued." I still tell myself that today. You should, too.

Our hearts are wired to have a deep, profound

relationship with God, who is our ultimate leader, our ultimate Father, and our guide. In Him, we are no longer inadequate, restless, lacking, or fearful. Instead, we are whole. We are more and more at peace and have a confidence that is born of firm knowledge that He is with us, and He won't let us fail.

Decide now if you believe there is a God who loves you, then define your fatherlessness, so you can begin to heal.

chapter three:

Symptoms of Fatherlessness

Symptoms of Fatherlessness

How do you know if you are experiencing fatherlessness? Of course, I lost my dad in a tragic accident and, suddenly, he was gone. I lost my father. Even still, it isn't always easy to realize your own fatherless journey. Whether you lost your father like I did (physical fatherlessness) or have an absentee father figure in your life (emotional fatherlessness), there is a sense of ignorance as you go through the negative motions—a carelessness in your life that makes you less aware of what you are so clearly going through.

To spot fatherlessness, there are four obvious symptoms, and I believe there is a chronological order to them as well—that the stages are sequential as they start to manifest themselves. I believe these symptoms are so crystal clear that you can even identify *where* a person is at in their fatherlessness journey. The four stages are isolation, anxiety, anger, and brokenness.

Isolation

Because you've already experienced so much hurt, you first begin to isolate yourself so there is less of a chance of experiencing more hurt. You think you can avoid further loss or absence of someone if you don't allow anybody to get in or get close in the first place. So you don't. The extrovert struggles with this, and they actually tend to just have damaged relationships in their wake, versus the introvert, who may struggle with real relationships altogether.

This is a scary stage for an introvert, because they already naturally internalize things. The way they think about the world is internal. And symptomatically, the people around them don't even pick up on their pain because there is less of a change in their persona. But these introverts can hurt tremendously inside as they go through this isolation phase because they literally isolate. It's the kid in high school who doesn't have any friendships, isn't social, or can't connect with anyone in the church group.

Furthermore, it's an incubating effect. Much like what the body does when it starts to fight a virus, you protect yourself from further hurt by shutting yourself down, by moving more slowly throughout life. But just like when you are sick, this process still robs you of so much energy. It takes a lot of energy spiritually and physically to deal with the loss of a father or the absence of one. And it hurts.

From isolation, depression and despondency are natural byproducts, because it's not healthy to be withdrawn or shut out from social structures. Ecclesiastes 4:10 and 12 talks about brotherhood and the jeopardy of isolation, saying, "For if they fall, one will lift up his fellow. But woe to him who is alone when he falls and has not another to lift him up! And though a man might prevail against one who is alone, two will withstand him—a threefold cord is not quickly broken." We are social beings because God made us that way, and men in particular wander in their loneliness. It feels so out of character.

Anxiety

Isolation can easily move into symptoms of anxiety, which implies no longer having a sense of direction. If you don't have a direction or purpose and feel like you no longer have anyone you can trust, then you internalize all your worries and anxiety sets in.

The opposite of being at peace is to be in a state of worry or anxiety. A person at this stage of fatherlessness could not possibly find any state of peace by leaning on their own understanding, because they literally feel lost. In the absence of an earthly father, they are physically gripped with fear and a timid spirit, where they are uncertain of themselves and of their ability to make conclusive decisions or move forward with anything in life, especially when it's relational. They are constantly asking themselves, How do I trust this person? And, moreover, What if I can't even count on myself to deliver to the people around me?

If I'm being perfectly honest with you, to this day, that is still an anxiety for me. I ask myself, What if I fail? What if I'm not up to the task? People who know me casually would be shocked to hear this, as I come across as very confident. But those who know me well can see that timid, uncertain man. Now, everybody experiences these fears at some point in life, but for a person going through fatherlessness and with nobody to affirm them, the answer to those questions can bring on tremendous fear. Virtual paralysis sets in, they don't engage with people, and their thought process is just to give up altogether. My grandmother always used to say that a stranger was a friend you just hadn't met yet, but I always struggled with believing that. I was far too fearful.

Anger

At this stage, you tell yourself, I can't do this. Especially when you've made harmful mistakes, you really start to self-loathe and beat yourself up. But those mistakes are born out of not having a good road map, foundation, or guide! In any case, you get angry with yourself and with those around you. You go into a defensive "victim" mode and blame others for your misfortune. This is in self-preservation, but it is extremely self-destructive behavior that hurts everyone around you. You've gone from isolation to anxiety and even depression to trying and failing, and now you are just angry and fed up. You may just want to lash out and run!

Typically, the anger will subside, but that could take years, so like any ongoing ailment, you learn to live with the hurt. The anger rears its ugly head under stress, yet you go on living with this pain, but you don't live effectively. And the byproduct of that is more harmful decisions that lead to further isolation, anxiety, and anger—and away we go with the downward spiral. Bad begets more bad, and you live over and over with the consequences of those harmful decisions. So what do you go back to? Isolation and hopelessness. You stay in that pool of muddy water. There is no fresh water coming in and no muddy water going out. It's just stagnant. How can you displace the muddy water?

In the absence of an answer, you get to a point where you can't see a way to live an effective life. Ironically, this is a sense of awareness that starts to take place, but instead of being aware of how to fix it, you simply become aware that it seems unfixable. You don't see a way to navigate toward a better way to engage in life, so you don't, and you resign to your fate. This is an acceptance of your brokenness.

In the absence of an answer, you get to a point where you can't see a way to live an effective life.

Brokenness

This is a sad point. When people resign to their brokenness, they live a corrupt, hurtful life. They communicate and see the world with resentment, and there is always contempt and a lack of satisfaction at play. Now, this resignation comes in different forms because we have different personalities, but either way, it manifests itself into some form of over-compensation. This person thinks, This is where I am broken and weak, so I'm actually going to over-compensate here with narcissism, control, addictions, or an unhealthy degree of success. But it is always reckless and fruitless.

To be honest, people at this stage live in their brokenness quite openly and around us all the time. In our churches, people arrive at our doorsteps broken, where often the church is their *last stop.* We have such an opportunity to give them the medicine they need, which is love. Instead, we expect them to conform to us rather than meeting them where they are, like Jesus did. We meet them instead with judgment and condemnation, so out the door they go, more disenfranchised with "the church" than even before. And what a missed opportunity! Often, we only get one chance to love a broken person before their walls return. But, when they compare themselves to other people, they see their brokenness, they don't know how to change it, so they resign to their fate, and an inadequate, default self takes over.

These four symptoms of fatherlessness are real,

visceral, and can be long-lasting if not properly dealt with. But there is another way. Luke says, "Ask, seek, and knock" (Luke 11:9), and you will find a righteous life. My translation of this for you is God saying, "Hey, man, I'm right here! If you simply ask of me, seek me, and come down on your knees to talk with me, I will help you. I will show you where you are broken. I will spend time with you. I will validate you as a man. I will heal your hurts. I will be your Father and much, much more, but you need to get real with me now." You are meant for great things, and now is your time.

You are meant for great things, and now is your time.

I know you already have a broken perception of fatherhood, and to suggest that there is a Father in heaven who loves you might not offer comfort. But healing can only come from Him who loves you, and you are worthy of His love.

A Letter to the Fatherless

Are you doing OK so far? I want to reach out and speak to you, because it's time. If you see yourself in this context, if you see yourself in those symptoms, do not resign yourself to this fate. You are valued tremendously, and you are enough! You can go from meaningless to mighty if you just say yes to a path toward healing. I know the path you are on—I was there, too—and now I can show you the way.

But first, you have to decide whether you want to continue on this broken road. This is your decision.

You have to decide whether you want to continue on this broken road.

But as you decide, you must know there is a God in heaven who loves you and totally wants to heal you and restore your life and relationships. He wants to help you overcome this marred identity and give you *hope,* something that eludes the fatherless like the sails of a distant vessel—you aren't even sure if it's real, *but it is.*

But God cannot give you hope without your permission. God is a gentleman, He is soft and kind and loving, and He cannot help you if you won't break from your isolation or give your anxieties to Him and give Him a chance. He is waiting for you to *want* to change.

The fatherless do not want to give anybody a chance. Can you blame them? They've already been hurt and broken, and the thought of that wound being tampered with—or worse, reopened—is unbearable. But, let me ask you, if there is even the remotest possibility that someone could show up back in the jungle—that someone could be there to guide you and have a map for you once again!—would you be open to that dialogue?

To that I say, what have you got to lose? You are already broken, you have already seen the consequences of your actions, your anger and despair. And, chances are that you have nothing but broken relationships, too. So why not give God a chance to help you?

The fatherless have a habit of being quitters. As James puts it in the Bible, "Alas, oh, God, reveal yourself to me, but there is not a determined effort." If you agree to this great and wonderful change, you must commit. Don't be lackadaisical about this! Make a decision, commit, and do not retreat. Retreating may have been your nature up until now, but you are not going to retreat anymore. You are only going to move forward.

He wants to help you overcome this marred identity and give you hope, something that eludes the fatherless like the sails of a distant vessel—you aren't even sure if it's real, *but it is.*

In *Unspoken Sermons,* George MacDonald wrote, "Who can give a man this, his own name? God alone." This is a process of initiation. You have been tested and triumphed, and now you must face your enemy and forge ahead with God as your advocate.

I was here once. Of course, I came to this fork in the road where I, too, needed to make a decision for myself. But first of all, I had to decide whether there was a God in heaven or not and if He loved me. From there, I had to decide whether or not I trusted Him. *But I knew I needed Him* to help me navigate. I needed Him to be my new guide, my new advocate in life, and now He can be in yours.

> Two roads diverged in a wood, and I —
> I took the one less traveled by,
> And that has made all the difference.
> (Robert Frost, "The Road Not Taken")

This is it. It will not be easy. To be vulnerable and willing is no easy task, and people are going to let you down along the way. The biggest trigger to make you want to retreat and resign yourself back into your brokenness is in the form of people—people who tell you that you are not good enough. Even people in the church—the very place you should go for support!—will let you down, and there will be moments of disappointment. But stay committed, because you will need that church body to grow in relationship with God and His Son Jesus. And trust, too, that within that church body, there are other broken people who might've been there for twenty years and still have not healed. But not you, because you are being deliberate, and you are going to heal.

Acknowledge your symptoms and trust in God. In no uncertain terms, there is a God who loves you—and you don't have to fully understand that at this point! But you do have to be open to it. Are you open to it? Are you willing to set a new course?

I have studied many times
The marble which was chiseled for me—
A boat with a furled sail at rest in a harbor.
In truth it pictures not my destination
But my life.
For love was offered me and I shrank from its disillusionment;
Sorrow knocked at my door, but I was afraid;
Ambition called to me, but I dreaded the chances.
Yet all the while I hungered for meaning in my life.
And now I know that we must lift the sail
And catch the winds of destiny
Wherever they drive the boat.
To put meaning in one's life may end in madness,
But life without meaning is the torture
Of restlessness and vague desire—
It is a boat longing for the sea and yet afraid.

(Edgar Lee Masters, *"George Gray"*)

Part Two

The Framework

chapter four:

Your Framework

Your Framework

"And I will give you a new heart, and a new spirit I will put within you. And I will remove the heart of stone from your flesh and give you a heart of flesh," Ezekiel 36:26.

To begin your healing, you need to know where you came from. What is your family's framework? Within your genealogy and upbringing are patterns and beliefs that can answer so much of who you are today.

Historically, we can learn so much from other people's mistakes. To move forward here, you have to take a hard look at your family's own belief systems that were passed down to you. In doing so, you will begin to see that you've got a pre-wired disposition, and what was once instilled in you as being fact was actually just *beliefs* predicated on bad foundations to begin with. You might need to rewire altogether, and this is not easy to realize or accept, but just like my father resigned to break his family's cycle of abuse, you have to concede and forgive those who handed you your framework and recognize that they were broken people as well. You are in a false start position, so to speak, but awareness of that position—be it true or not—is how you correctly begin the path to healing and to an honest relationship with God.

You can be a pioneer in your family.

If you want to get on the right path, you need to first admit that you are on the wrong path, and it's OK that your family set you on that wrong path. They never dealt with their brokenness—I know my dad was trying!—but I did deal with my brokenness, and you can, too. You can be a pioneer in your family.

It begins with acceptance of who our family once was. I remember my dad's best friend saying to me after my dad died, "Your dad had some great qualities. Take the good, and throw away the bad." If your family has positive qualities, thank God for those, thank your parents for those, and build on that. Those good characteristics that your parents or grandparents passed down to you are likely *your* strengths today. Work from those. For example, my dad was always big on follow-through, and that's a blessing for me today, because even when I had a hard time trying to fix my broken road, I was *determined* to finish. I took my strengths given to me by my dad and applied it to overcoming my fatherlessness.

On the other hand, you must acknowledge and work with any negative generational lessons, too, and then choose a different path. For whatever reason, my dad came up short, and I let that harden me for a long time. But then I identified it, and instead of building from his negative mindset or beliefs and letting them be part of me, too, *I chose a different way.* And that's where God comes in. Whereas we have the framework from positive qualities and can continue on those paths, we aren't going to have the framework when we step away from our family's negative qualities, because we are starting a *new path.* So God comes in to fill that gap, and He gives you a new playbook. For you, He paves that new way.

Deuteronomy 31:8 says, "The Lord himself goes before you. He will be with you; he will not leave you or forsake you. Do not fear or be dismayed." We are allowing God to enter into our lives as a mentor and a guide to help us heal.

A Call to Build

If you are ready to either change or move forward with your framework, you must begin by respecting the source of your fatherlessness. If your father is physically absent like mine, you don't really have to worry about putting in any buffers on belief systems that were wrong or pushed onto you, because your father is gone. It's easier to rewrite your script in this case, because you don't have anyone forcing a wrong script onto you at the same time.

However, if you have an absentee father who

may still physically be present in your life, you have to adopt a new belief system without rejecting your absentee father. You have to navigate forgiveness of your earthly father while he is still in and out of your life. He may be trying to inject a certain belief system into your life that you know is wrong, but the trick is to acknowledge that it's wrong and still love him anyway.

In order for you to move forward, *you must reject the belief or the idea, not the person.*

In order for you to move forward, *you must reject the belief or the idea, not the person.*

When your absentee dad is still in the picture, this is hard because you are trying to identify where your dad came up short while he is still with you, continually coming up short. Once you recognize it, it is easier to be deliberate with what you accept and what you reject, but it's almost more frustrating, too, because now that you've become aware, you can't believe how badly your parents taught you for as long as they did! In any case, you have to be careful here that you continue to love this person and reject only his beliefs.

You might even have to limit or buffer your father's access to your life. Because if he has yet to identify his own failure, he's surely resigned to that life—it's well entrenched, and you can by no means expect him to change. He doesn't see anything wrong with himself; he is completely unaware! So sometimes it's best to keep your distance from him while you rebuild your framework so as not to be deterred.

And give him grace. As you continue to engage with him in some way or another, your goal will now be to subtly influence him in a reverse way as a son to a father. Your actions are saying, "I love you for where you are at in your walk." You have to acknowledge in grace that, for whatever reason, God has ahold of you now, the scales have been lifted from your eyes, and the only thing battling against you is a father who didn't teach you well and who may likely now be threatened by your growth.

If you see that he is threatened, continue to give him grace, focus on the good you can have with him, and walk with him. Reject his false beliefs, but love him anyway. Perhaps, love him more than ever before.

But it's not enough to just say that I'm going to act with grace and keep a distance. You really have to create structure around those relationships. Even for me, my dad was gone, but I've had to create a ton of structure around the *memories* of my dad, because he was still an influencer in my life for fifteen years. With all these memories, I still had to create thought behaviors to buffer my dad, even though I love him and miss him tremendously. I needed to create a healthy boundary as I built my new framework, even with a deceased parent.

As you work, surround yourself with a loving church and people who can freely demonstrate the love of Christ, who are going to root for you and with whom you can be broken. Find a third, godly party with whom you talk through these things and express intent. Because you need to be deliberate! You cannot just give those negative belief systems a nod and move on. You need to really articulate it. Maybe you write it down or talk it out with others, but you really need to flush this out to feel new again.

To break these generational strongholds, you need to be open to a power greater than your own. God can help you defeat prior belief systems! You can move forward with grace and be deliberate about breaking the pattern if you allow Him to create in you a heart of flesh (Ezek. 36:26). Up until now, you've been stagnant in muddy waters. If you want clean water, you've got to empty out the dirty water and make room. And you can. Let this be your first glass of fresh water. Let this be clear. Learn from the past, and move forward in your *own* framework.

chapter five:

Forgiveness

Forgiveness

"We rejoice in our sufferings, knowing that suffering produces endurance, and endurance produces character, and character produces hope, and hope does not put us to shame, because God's love has been poured into our hearts through the Holy Spirit who has been given to us. For while we were still weak, at the right time Christ died for the ungodly. For one will scarcely die for a righteous person—though perhaps for a good person one would dare even to die— but God shows his love for us in that while we were still sinners, Christ died for us," Romans 5:3-8.

Forgiveness is a state of the heart, not of the mind.

To move forward in grace means that we must forgive. For both physical and emotional fatherlessness, we must forgive our fathers for their actions or lack thereof, and we must forgive *ourselves* for harboring any anger, fear, or resentment. We must be set free, and forgiveness is key.

Forgiveness is a state of the heart, not of the mind. Forgiveness is important—not just surrounding your earthly father, but in life as a whole—and it allows us to reclaim and affirm who we are as men. But you cannot forgive others if you can't forgive yourself, and you definitely cannot accept God's forgiveness if you can't even forgive yourself first.

But I know, it's hard. Forgiveness is a funny beast. It is one of the hardest hurdles for us as human beings, but Jesus talks tremendously about it. He tells us to pray, to forgive those who trespass against us (Matt. 6) so that He can forgive us of our sins. In Matthew 18:21-22, Peter came to Jesus and asked, "'Lord, how often will my brother sin against me, and I forgive him? As many as seven times?' And Jesus said to him, 'I do not say to you seven times, but seventy times seven.'"

I believe that true forgiveness is something unique only to Christians who truly know their Father. It is not a familiar feat, especially when we don't have the natural inclination to forgive while in our brokenness, but it is possible.

I believe that forgiveness is the ability to carry on and interact with the source of the hurt. Forgiveness has nothing to do with the person you are forgiving. I can only control what I do. And when I choose to forgive, I am saying the only thing I feel toward you is love, compassion, and a desire to see you not continue in your pain.

Forgiveness is not judgment, elitism, or superiority. Instead, there is a real seasoning of grace. You know you have forgiven someone if you can genuinely pray for them. You are no longer pulled into their world of brokenness. Even though you still care about a good outcome for them, you are trusting God in that, not your own abilities.

For men, this is difficult, because we are used to fixing things ourselves. But resist that desire, step away from your efforts, and give it to God. Pastor Knowles says to me often, "Jonathan, God is painting a beautiful canvas, but you have your nose pressed into it. You can't see what He is doing because you are just too close. If you take a breath and pull yourself back, the painting will start to reveal itself. As your vision adjusts, God will give you new eyes and a new perspective."

Resentment—or choosing not to forgive—is like drinking poison and waiting for the other person to die.

If you have truly forgiven someone, when you interact with them, you see their brokenness and the injury they inflicted on you with compassion, not resentment. It is unhealthy for us to harbor resentment. Resentment—or choosing not to forgive—is like drinking poison and waiting for the other person to die. There is no healing in resentment. There is only healing in forgiveness.

In his message on facing the giant of forgiveness, Dr. David Jeremiah tells us that resentment never stays the same. It grows and distorts reality and keeps you chained to the past. It is like a bad air that pollutes not only the bitter person, but everyone they come into contact with (davidjeremiah.org). Moreover, people today think they can keep their bitterness to themselves, but the problem with that is these people are held hostage to their resentment, and everything around them is negatively influenced without them even realizing this. When you carry bitterness in your soul, you allow yourself to be imprisoned by your past. And if the bitterness is prolonged, it becomes a burden you cannot live without. Truly, in time, the hate will no longer belong to you, *you will belong to the hate,* and it will consume your heart.

When you carry bitterness in your soul, you allow yourself to be imprisoned by your past.

If you cannot forgive your earthly father, your Heavenly Father has no room to be in relationship with you. Forgiveness displaces resentment and fills your heart with love, the way it did for me.

When an absentee father hurts someone, the world tells them to just write that father off, but that means the wound will never heal. If you want the wound to heal, you actually have to stay in that person's life and get to a complete place of deliverance in terms of forgiveness. This doesn't mean letting that person continue to hurt you emotionally or physically. But there is a work that needs to be done in your heart. And, amazingly, if there is any chance for that person to heal, it will be when they see you do it.

There are two steps to forgiveness: Stop, and pray.

Stop

The first thing you need to do is get some space. Step away. You need rest. You are angry, bitter and frustrated, and you cannot move forward in that. And it's OK to step away and get clarity! When you do that, you can start to fill your cup with something different.

Now, this doesn't mean to physically step away. Remember, if you are experiencing emotional fatherlessness, you are not to reject the person. Instead, you are to keep him in your life at a distance, and in the case of forgiveness, you simply need to emotionally disengage for a time while you embrace the circumstance and find peace in it.

Give yourself refuge from the relationship, give yourself time to sort through your thought process, and get in a better headspace. The source of your fatherlessness will want predictability in your behavior—this change will be threatening, remember—but this forgiveness is for *your* framework, not theirs.

Pray

Then, you can pray. Take some time, however you understand it, to talk to God. Allow me to encourage you. There is a God who loves you, and He is listening. The Bible can be intimidating, but you can start with some good reading material that parallels the Bible and helps you to better understand who God is.

You can go to God in your brokenness. He doesn't expect you to get cleaned up. After graduating from a yearlong addictions program, a young woman from Teen Challenge shared in her testimony, "God loves you just the way you are. He just doesn't want to leave you that way." That hit me square in the chest!

Your prayer is a confession of your brokenness. You are getting authentic and real with your Father in heaven for the first time. And authenticity with God is important because it encourages you to be authentic and transparent with *yourself.* If you communicate with profanity, you don't have to hold any punches with God. *Get real with God!* And let go of your pride. In men, pride is such a weakness, but if you are not prepared to approach God in humility, it's a nonstarter. Pastor Louie Giglio said, "Humility is the currency of heaven." What powerful yet counter-cultural words for the fatherless, men who have thus far held so desperately to pride as a safety blanket! But you are acknowledging that God is in control, letting Jesus rewrite the script of your life and putting your trust in Him.

The first thing you should pray for is to be introduced to someone who can come alongside you. Ask for someone who can show God's love to you and demonstrate forgiveness. This is about accountability—you will need people who love and care for you and want to pray with you as you let your hurt go and begin to forgive. Pray that God will bring them into your life, and then invite them in.

As you begin to engage with your Father in heaven, there will be an element of fear in you that will tell you to stop. Deny that fear, and move forward in your relationship with God. Then, as you continue to move forward, add ceremony to your forgiveness. Write down the hurts and the wrongs, and ceremoniously destroy it or burn it to truly let it go. I believe you must see it and then see it be destroyed to realize why you were holding onto it before. Release the hurt in any way you can.

You, too, must face your monster. If you want to achieve forgiveness.

When I was on my journey toward forgiveness, I had to go back to the place where I suffered deep loss. I had to go back to the waters where my fatherlessness began, and I had to come to peace with God. I struggled so much with *why* God would do this to my family, so I knew the only way to find peace was to go to the same place where the pain was caused.

Today, it is a place of peace, and I know there is victory for me over that. I just go there, and I pray. I could take you there, to this very place of tragedy—where I see so many divers out there every time I go!—and I could sit there for hours in total peace. That is forgiveness.

You, too, must face your monster. If you want to achieve forgiveness—if you want to build a framework and move on—you must step away, pray to God, and find your peace.

Believe me when I say, you deserve and you need this peace more than you know.

chapter six:
Finding Your Allies

Finding Your Allies

Community plays an important role as you begin to rebuild your framework. You need support, a fan club, cheerleaders, accountability, demonstration of healthy relationships, for starters. You need people in your life who know how to live in a way that's different from what you've experienced and have been immersed in up until now. You need to know where the well is with the fresh water, because you are not used to going to it, but they will take you there.

Now, when you begin to engage in community, you may initially feel intimidated, especially in the "traditional church." There will be discomfort. If you felt inadequate before, those demons will really haunt you now, and you will feel even *more* out of your comfort zone. Yes, it is unfamiliar territory, and you will feel very unsure about a lot of things you once felt certain about. Everything will be rattled, but don't be alarmed! I tell you all this so that I can plead, do not recoil, do not fall into that fear we talked about, do not retreat behind your "castle walls." Just keep weighing into it. Even if it feels foreign right now, embrace it, and *keep going.*

When you are not used to having a sense of security, your guard is up because it seems too good to be true. You will find yourself thinking, Is this real? Are these people authentic? And that skepticism is okay. Because soon, you will realize that this community you are trying to engage with has seen their own time in the trenches. They, too, have had struggles to overcome, but the moment that vulnerability commences, just slide into it and pray for more of that. Pray for more interaction with people like that in your community.

As you slowly engage, do not beat yourself up for making mistakes. Instead, acknowledge when you stumble, then brush yourself off and keep going. You are like a newborn babe, man! And it's OK to stumble here, because you are among a group of people who are supportive, empathetic, and want to see you succeed. So embrace the falls, embrace the love around you, and keep it up.

God wants us to be part of a community.

Being a Christian today, we often hear that it's hard and it's lonely, but I don't believe that was God's will for us. God wants us to be part of a community. He wants us to have fellowship, especially for prayer. When you face adversity or struggles, it's important to know that there are other people out there who are not only cheering for you but are going to God and asking Him to move His hand in your circumstances. You deserve to live in a community where people are praying for you; you just have to make the choice to engage!

Yes, sometimes Christianity can feel lonely, but I believe you have to go through a period of loneliness as you build an intimate relationship with God. I think you need to take some time to get alone with God. Jesus spent time praying alone, but He also had community, and you should, too.

Who Are Your People?

To more easily digest this overwhelming sense of community, I want to help you break down different levels of community that will be important to you. Instead of walking out your door one day, seeking community and expecting to feel engaged, I want to intentionally break down for you the meaning of "community" into four different groups I encourage you to find.

But take caution here. In the previous chapter, we talked about asking God to introduce you to someone who can come alongside you. And that is how you will begin to find your community, but you also have to pray here that the *wrong* person doesn't present themselves either. I've learned that if you are praying for one thing, it seems without fail that the devil will try to present you with really well-disguised, close-to-the-mark alternatives at every turn, so pray, too, for a discerning heart.

Discernment means really asking yourself in the face of a new friend, Does this person care about me getting off this road? Does this person care about me genuinely, authentically finding God? And, do they have a deep understanding of God's nature? Do they have people around *them* suggesting that as well? Discernment is examining your intended direction before proceeding.

When I served in the military, I was in the artillery, and when you try to hit a target, you triangulate the target by zeroing in on it. To do that, you preferably had three or at least two points of reference. In discernment, the same is true. If you can confirm it with God's Word, feel it in your prayer life, and have someone else validate that this may be or may not be a good direction for you, then you have positively discerned a potential relationship. Discernment is about more than decision making, it is taking time to understand where God is leading you. Discernment is thoughtful patience while moving forward. Psalm 46:10 says, "Be still, and know that I am God."

This is a new muscle for the fatherless, because you are starting to develop a relationship with God you've never really experienced before. You learn to let God offer you feedback, and admittedly, there is a level of fear associated with discernment because you are conceding that you are not going to make the decision yourself. You are instead going to tune in to what God wants for you.

Up until now, you may have had many good friends, many of whom will continue to be in your life, but I call these fair-weather friendships. You can't hang your hat on them. In my own life, I've gotten very good at discerning a fair-weather friend versus someone who genuinely cares about the end game for my family and I. I'm asking you to do the same here. If you are ready to rebuild your framework and welcome a new community into your life, you might just want to invite anybody in to feel supported, but get this right. Seek community via these four different groups, and discern each relationship as it's introduced to you, whether it is healthy for you and will help you continue to move in a positive direction.

God will honor your commitment, and with His help, you can do this.

And don't get discouraged. My wife and I prayed for supportive fellowship for years before we found it. Until then, read your Bible, and find a good church. God will honor your commitment, and with His help, you can do this.

One-on-one Mentorship

A one-on-one mentorship is a relationship with someone who is confident in their own spiritual journey.

They are a sage—not necessarily older than you, but they are certainly more mature in their relationship with God. But let's be honest—at this point in your journey, *everybody* is going to be more mature than you in their relationship with God, right? There is no need for discernment here, it's pretty obvious that this person is opposite to you!

They are a sage—not necessarily older than you, but they are certainly more mature in their relationship with God.

Ironically, this is probably already a person in your life, but one you've perhaps mocked up until now or even had an element of disdain for. Now, however, you see their strengths in a new light—they are strong where you are weak, and you need them. If you don't know how to love, this mentor can demonstrate an equal, *opposite* amount of love while also demonstrating superiority wherever you are weak, and you are OK with that.

This mentor can relate to you—not with sympathy, but with empathy—and they have a sincere love for you, their mentee. There is also an element of shared experiences. Regardless if this mentor has been through what you are going through, they have the ability to meet you where you are at and in a genuine, nonjudgmental and loving way.

This mentor will hold you accountable and help you to focus on the things that matter to you now. And that has a real, profound impact, because when you finally have someone who cares about you, you don't want to let them down. Remember John Eldredge's important question, "Do I have what it takes?" With a mentor, you now have somebody who is investing in you and willing to say, *yes!* You *do* have what it takes! Especially for a young man, there is a deep desire not to let that mentor down.

One-on-one mentorship is huge for the fatherless because they begin to not feel alone anymore. Way back in the beginning, when I was seventeen years old after my dad's death and facing fatherlessness for the first time, I felt so alone. Now, I'm not alone! I have people I can talk to and rely on, and I feel heard. For someone who is coming off a broken road, to feel that is critical. It is monumental, and it is a great first step in finding your new community.

Peer Group

For the fatherless, you want an expanded group of co-mentees. These are men who are at the same place—or maybe just slightly ahead—of where you are in your relationship with God. Just like you, they are still raw and rough, but with them you can be vulnerable, and you can grow together. This is a group of men who are all at the same developmental step in their faith, but everyone is clear on the fact that they do not want to go back to that broken road, so they support one another. They are in it together, ready to call you out if you try to withdraw or isolate. They are like brothers.

Everyone in this peer group has a one-on-one mentorship like you do, but while your mentors are strong and mature in their relationship with God and you are learning from them, this is a group of friends who know they are broken and want to know God. And even though you have accountability with your mentor, this is even further, internal accountability, because you are meeting with these guys at least once a week and are integrating them into your day-to-day life.

With a peer group, it's harder for you to stray now because you have a support system through multiple men who are checking in with you and expecting you to check in on them. You are actively learning together, sharing together, encouraging one another, and helping others together. I never grew up with brothers, so I experienced something new in my own peer groups, and it felt like what I imagined having a brother would feel like, and it was nice.

Your peer group needs to be at least three or four guys and no more than seven. Otherwise, it gets too diluted, and the introverts in the room won't speak up. There needs to be a level of intimacy that you aren't used to but you know you need. It's uncomfortable at first, but it is necessary. It's also necessary that it's only men (and for women's peer groups to only be made up of women), as we are most likely to be vulnerable and honest with the same sex. When it comes to taboo topics like pornography, men aren't likely to discuss openly if there is a woman in the room, whereas, if they are alone with men, they can more openly discuss their problems.

Let me give you further context. Recently, I felt compelled to begin my own peer group. As a Christian running a company with predominantly non-Christians working for me, I began to feel very alone when trying to live out Christian values. I felt like I didn't have anyone with whom I could talk about my business and about being a Christian leader in the business world, so I started a prayer leadership breakfast, and it still exists today. I invite Christian men in places of leadership, and we get together about every six weeks so as not to disrupt everyone's hectic schedules, and the guys really like it. We meet for an hour and a half, we open in prayer, and then we talk about our struggles. It's very loose, vulnerable conversation, and this is an example of a peer group.

Community of Believers

I'm reluctant to call this a church community. If I've observed anything in the past seven years, it's that the biggest issue with the North American church is that it's turned into a bit of a spiritual spa. A church that only ministers to itself is much more of a "community hall" than it is a church community, and if that church isn't outwardly focused on community—the lonely, hungry, widowed, elderly, and orphaned—then they are no church at all. Let's call it what it is!

So I'm not suggesting that you seek out a church community. I'm telling you to find a community of believers *within* a church community, people within a certain congregation who chase community passionately. They are physically out there, engaged in their neighbors' lives. James was an early leader in the church in Jerusalem just after Jesus was crucified, and I think He put it best when He said, "What good is it, my brothers, if someone says he has faith but does not have works? Can that faith save him? If a brother or a sister is poorly clothed and lacking in daily food, and one of you says to them, 'Go in peace, be warmed and be filled,' without giving them the things needed for the body, what good is that? So also faith by itself, if it does not have works, is dead. But someone will say, 'You have faith, and I have works.' Show me your faith apart from your works, and I will show you my faith by my works" (James 2:14-18).

"What good is it, my brothers, if someone says he has faith but does not have works? Can that faith save him?"

Let me declare to you, we cannot be idle if we

follow Jesus. We must want to take action for our community and do good, and we must surround ourselves with people who are eager to take action with us. This is your community of believers.

Now, this will not be easy to find. There are 364,000 churches in America alone and 70 million people who call themselves Christians so, to be blunt, you will need to do some sifting. There is absolutely some discernment at work here! You will need to pray, "Lord, give me discernment and lead me to a place where I can serve." It also is not enough to simply walk into a church, read their mission statement and figure out if they are a community of servants. Surely, if their mission statement does not include going out and reaching the masses, then you know that's a bad starting point, or if in their Sunday morning fliers there is no mention about working at the soup kitchen on Friday. But even so, within that church there can be people whose heart cry is truly community engagement, and *that* is who you should gravitate toward. Be like them.

Like your mentor, a community of believers is mature in their faith. They are fed and ready to go out and feed others. So this type of community is further down your path of healing, but when building your relationship with God, it is critical to serve and to be around others who want to serve. Have a servant's heart.

The People You Pour Into

When your community becomes strong—no matter how long that takes—you can begin to pour into others and share your love for God. The gospel of Jesus could not be any clearer: Love your neighbor, and share Jesus' love for them. As you grow from being on your broken road, surely you will see the amazing gospel at work in your own life. You will see and feel the transformation, so what a shame to then *not* go out and love others and share that narrative and miracle that is taking place in your own life! How could you not?

When you pour into other people, there is also an element of growth in your own faith. It takes you to an entirely different level that is difficult to even articulate it is so powerful, but it's there, and you feel it. I've often said the greatest gift one can receive is the gift of giving, but I think it's way more than that. C.S. Lewis said, "There are no ordinary people. You have never talked to a mere mortal" (*The Weight of Glory,* C.S. Lewis). Wow! Every interaction we have, Jesus is there. And when we pour into others, we are being Jesus to that person.

There is something very humbling about giving. When you pour into others, any pride you had starts to melt away, and it feels good. Evangelist David Wilkerson spoke in a sermon once about how everyone is like a stray dog. We are all running around with a bone in our mouths that has no meat on it, he explained, and we think that bone is as good as it gets, because it's all we have. But the gospel of Jesus is like a steak, and if we want the dog to put down the bone, someone needs to offer him a steak. That is us pouring into others, giving people something better than they've ever tasted before.

For me, I just come full boar now. A friend said to me, "Jonathan, one of your greatest gifts is evangelism." I know that has a negative connotation, but I realize now that a true evangelist's heart is an apostle without shame, just sharing God's love with passion, vigor, excitement, and enthusiasm, and for me, that just cannot be curbed. I am there! Even as I share this book with you now, it is not enough to proclaim my joy! Jesus said, "The kingdom of heaven is like treasure hidden in a field, which a man found and covered up. In his joy he goes and sells all that he has and buys that field" (Matt. 13:44). Don't let the "traditional church" steal that joy from you! To be a Christian is a deliberate choice. If you have an opportunity to serve but you don't go, you are literally squandering an amazing gift, then allowing it to wither and die on the vine. Don't let the dormancy of an inactive church

---

He has been working on this puzzle for over 2,000 years and right now, at this time in history, He has you set to do something.

---

community steal your vigor!

I believe that God is making a puzzle. He has been working on this puzzle for over 2,000 years and right now, at this time in history, He has you set to do something. Right now is the time that your skills, your energy, and your relationships are all for a purpose. I find it remarkable that people can have this coming about, where they can get themselves off their broken road, find God, find their support systems and then pour into others. What a beautiful miracle and transformation … that is happening within you.

chapter seven:

Your Father

Your Father

When I was six years old, my dad was running a construction company. I remember one Saturday morning, I wanted to go to work with him, but he didn't want to take me. Even my mom had said, "Wayne, just take him with you!" But Dad was grumbling. "No, he will just get in the way," he said, "I have a lot to do, and I don't want him under foot." I was just beside myself about this. I was this classic, six-year-old little red-headed kid, and I was pleading with him, "I won't get in the way!" I was *determined* to spend time with my dad. So what did I do? I went out to his truck, unbeknownst to him, reached up and opened the passenger door and then kept it open *just enough* so that when he finally agreed to let me go, I could just run out and grab the door myself instead of him having to take the time to open the door for me and let me in. I was determined to maximize my time with my dad *that much* and not be left behind on the day's adventure.

Anyway, Dad capitulated! Mom convinced him

to let me go, and I remember him saying, "Alright, c'mon on, boy, come with me." So we walked out to the driveway, and instead of me running to my passenger door that I had so conveniently already set ajar for myself, Dad put his arm around me, took me around to the driver's side, opened the door and told me to climb on in. And because I was so excited, I had completely forgotten that I left the passenger door open for myself! Instead, I was just sitting proud as a peacock up on my knees, playing with the radio and ready to go. But as Dad backed out of the driveway, I leaned against the side door and fell right out. Dad said the last thing he saw was my feet going out the door! So he reached across to grab me as he slammed on the brakes, and I was literally under the truck as the truck came to a stop with the tire right over my head!

My Dad almost ran me over that day because I was so desperate to be with him. I know he felt tremendously convicted as a dad after that, for his son to want to be with him that badly, but I tell you this story because I think this is how we should love our Father. Today, I do feel this way, like a six-year-old kid who just wants to get in the truck and be with God. I can't wait to work with my heavenly Dad! I feel the same adoration and euphoria, and this is what I want for you, too.

Who is God as Father?

Regardless of how well-versed you are in the Bible, I find the Parable of the Lost Son a great starting place in terms of understanding who our Father is (Luke 15). Jesus does an amazing job of not only characterizing the Lost Son but of showing us that he had a repenting heart when the son goes to his father and says, "I have sinned against heaven and before you" (Luke 15:18). But what I love most about the Parable of the Lost Son is the *father*. Luke, in verse 20 says, "But while he was still a long way off, his father saw him and felt compassion." Now this son was probably fearful about coming home after leaving his father and squandering his wealth, but the father's response is what every man desperately yearns for—and I believe a man's heart leaps when he reads this—that the father was so filled with compassion that he "ran and embraced him and kissed him."

And then, the father restored his son! "But the father said to his servants, 'Bring quickly the best robe, and put it on him, and put a ring on his hand, and shoes on his feet. And bring the fattened calf and kill it, and let us eat and celebrate. For this my son was dead, and is alive again; he was lost, and is found.' And they began to celebrate" (Luke 15:22-24). How giving of the son's father to not hold anything against him or greet him in anger but to instead celebrate his return and show him all his love! I believe this is how we should perceive our Father in heaven. No matter where you've been, He is waiting to adorn you in the best robe and honor you with a feast and celebration. Ever patiently, He waits for you.

Psalm 68:5 says, "Father of the fatherless and protector of widows is God in his holy habitation." God's nature as demonstrated in that verse is absolute compassion, engagement and a desire to be reunited with you as a son. In no uncertain terms, He is saying that He is your Father, you are never alone, and He has compassion for you. And when in relationship with Him, you will be inspired, and you will inspire others. It doesn't matter if you are in a prison cell, in a cubicle or atop the highest mountain or lowest valley, God has a purpose for you and wants to totally wrap His arms around you so that you can inspire others. Your story is worth something! He promises to help you. *He is for you.*

God wants to build you up and send you out. His engagement in your life is to literally say, "I believe in you, welcome back, here is everything you need, now let's go." He wants to celebrate you in relationship with Him, then arm you so you can be who He intended you to be. He wants to put you to work.

Your story is worth something! He promises to help you. *He is for you.*

God does not want you sitting on a couch playing video games or drinking beer with your buddies. He doesn't want you to commiserate about the rut you find yourself in life. Instead, He wants you out in the field, helping Him to create something that is long-lasting. He wants you to work and, fortunately, our nature as men is to go to work!

He wants you to work and, fortunately, our nature as men is to go to work!

When men are idle, they moan and whine and complain. (Why do we call it man colds, right?!) We are the worst possible, and it's brutal! But I truly believe this is because the only way men are strong is when they are working. Men are built for heavy lifting and physical labor, and the toughness comes from the work. A man's mind needs something to focus on, and a man's body needs something to physically do. Why wouldn't we want to respect God's intention for our bodies to be out in the community and working?

Who are We as His Son?

When we are in relationship with God as His Son, we live a life of purpose on purpose. I wake up every morning to say, "Lord, you gave me this day. Give me the outlet to be the man You want me to be."

When a man is not yet a son of God, he has a timidity about him. He is fearful, hesitant, unsure, and not the leader we think of when we think of the man. But when a man does have sonship with God, he has purpose. Remember James 2, "Show me your faith apart from your works, and I will show you my faith by my works." A man in sonship has no fear, and he is motivated to act. If you have true sonship, you are not content to get up in the morning and *not* go to work for your Father. Rather, it is an honor, you are excited and you cannot wait to see what the two of you are going to accomplish together that day. This is a real shift in your mentality! But this is the euphoric adoration I experienced as a son with my earthly father, and this is my hope for you with our Heavenly Father.

Life of purpose on purpose.

When you begin to truly open up to God as a Father, you will first experience fear. Up until now, you have had this preconceived idea of who your Father is, or maybe you didn't have one at all, and now you are trying to get to a place where you need to trust Him, and that's just another hurdle to overcome. You will likely ask yourself, What if you let me down? What if this ends like it did with my earthly father? This fear can cause paralysis, but don't let it!

When I came to know God, I had deep fear that I wasn't good enough. Even when you do commit, you wonder if you are just kidding yourself. This is why you need sonship with Jesus, because that relationship will bring you to your knees, where you pray for strength.

Wake up early, go for a jog, do whatever it is you need to do, and pray through the fear. "Lord, I give this to you. You know my heart. I believe you will honor this because I'm doing this out of love for you." Understand that your fears are there only so you can begin to trust. Psalm 139:23-24 says, "Search me, O God, and know my heart! Try me and know my thoughts. And see if there be any grievous way in me, and lead me in the way everlasting."

It might feel like a dog and pony show. Two steps forward and one step back. But like Pastor Lennett Anderson says, "Our past is a place of reference, not of residence" (StarMetro Halifax newspaper, 2016). In time, you will begin to overcome the fear, and then, the trust will build so much that instead of praying through fear, you now are praying in faith, "I trust you. I will step forward because I know you will catch me." What a transformation to move forward from fear to trust! Hebrews 13:5 says, "I will never leave you nor forsake you." This is true sonship with God.

Hebrews 13:5 says, "I will never leave you nor forsake you."

I believe Lamentations 3 was written for all men in their brokenness. I still return to it to this day and every time feel so overwhelmed by its message. It begins in hurt. "I am the man who has seen affliction under the rod of his wrath; he has driven and brought me into darkness without any light; surely against me he turns his hand again and again the whole day long. He has made my flesh and skin waste away; he has broken my bones. He has besieged and enveloped me with bitterness and tribulation" (vv. 1-5).

There is so much pain here that we can relate to! But then, as it continues, it's about momentous healing. "The steadfast love of the LORD never ceases; his mercies never come to an end; they are new every morning; great is your faithfulness. 'The LORD is my portion,' says my soul, 'therefore I will hope in him' " (vv. 22-24).

This is ultimate healing. I am going to trust that it doesn't make sense to me why I've endured my brokenness, because I am saved by faith (Rom. 4). And I also know that my alternative is to go back to my broken road. And we know that broken road! It's a dead end, there is nothing on it! I choose faith and sonship with God instead. Do you?

It does not matter who you are. We all have shortcomings. But to have a healthy self-awareness of that inadequacy is balance. When we are in sonship with God, we first experience fear, then we build trust, and, lastly, we create balance. You will begin to admit that you can only do so much in a day and that we as humans are limited. For me, it's getting to a point where I know I don't need to strive anymore as His son. My striving was once to compensate for my sense of inadequacy, and I was very alone in that. But now, it's almost like I can rest so peacefully that I can hear, "Jonathan, do you trust me?"

We live in a chaotic world that demands a five-year plan, a ten-year plan and so on, but in relationship with God, I kind of like not having a five-year plan. The book of James says that it doesn't mean anything if it's not God's plan. Of course, I'm still going to live with intention and put my best foot forward, but I'm also going to allow God to redirect as He sees fit.

Balance is still working hard and being resourceful, but it's knowing that it's not all up to you anymore.

Balance is still working hard and being resourceful, but it's knowing that it's not all up to you anymore. Instead of compensating or striving, you are working on stuff that feeds your soul, which means you have arrived to your purpose and you are doing what God equipped you to do. "I am fearfully and wonderfully made" (Psalm 139:14).

A New Way of Life

In Psalm 51, David is writing in the wake of his own adultery and is desperate to be close to God again. He writes, "Purge me with hyssop, and I shall be clean; wash me, and I will be whiter than snow. Let me hear joy and gladness, let the bones that you have broken rejoice" (vv. 7-8). In my own sin, I was lost and didn't feel the Holy Spirit. I was completely separated from God, and it was a horrible feeling! But then, David goes on to say, "Create in me a clean heart, O God, and renew a right spirit within me. Cast me not away from your presence and take not your Holy Spirit from me. Restore to me the joy of your salvation, and uphold me with a willing spirit" (vv. 10-12). I am no longer that dead body, I am alive! And, because I am reinvigorated with my purpose in life, I can minister and pour into others my love for Jesus. I can be the son that God called me to be.

When I look at my past now, I see in no uncertain terms that I was living for myself. I was winning and keeping score; it was selfish and there was nothing transcendent about it. Now, I see that the only value in whatever success I have in life is that I can use it for helping others and influencing people by drawing them to Jesus' truth.

When in relationship with God as Father, you are filled just as much as you were empty. You are now living in victory, confidence, trust in Him, with purpose and hope, and you are deliberate in your actions and loving people like you never could before. And the more you pour yourself out, the fuller your cup is. You are increasingly surrounded by people who love your energy, love

The more you pour yourself out, the fuller your cup is.

your camaraderie and your transcendent glow. Most importantly, you have a purpose and objective in life that goes beyond just making a living. When you fill your days with purpose, you yourself begin to feel fulfilled. You can go to work with your Father! Sonship with God feels a lot like that. How are you going to maximize your time with your Heavenly Father?

Part Three

The Life

chapter eight:
Husbandhood

Husbandhood

"Husbands, love your wives, as Christ loved the church and gave himself up for her," *Ephesians 5:25.*

I am bold to proclaim this, but I do not think husbands today are doing a very good job. We talked earlier how in fatherlessness, there is a lack of confidence and a sudden need to defer to others for strength. And I think for husbands, it's easy to defer to their wives, so they do. But what happens is that they then leave their wives carrying a disproportionate amount of burden in their family. Their wives are suddenly taking on child rearing, finances, the home and, meanwhile, the husbands are living like boys in their wives' homes. They are not purposeful, they are not proactive, and they are not engaged.

When a fatherless husband has no model to follow or no definition of what true husbandhood should be, marriages are strained. A family can still exist, but it doesn't flourish. Over-burdened wives feel unloved, lonely, and inadequate, and the husbands are idle. What's worse is that if these husbands have sons, the son follows suit and they, too, start to model idle behavior.

I will go so far as to say that husbands today have a lack of respect for their wives and children. When I see a man treating his wife with disdain or contempt, it really, really bothers me. And I don't understand this! How can a man take his wife for granted and not appreciate this amazing gift and responsibility that God has given him? Now, I speak out of failure here, but there is no way I am going to make that mistake again in the future. We must prioritize the relationship we have been given with our wives, and we must be deliberate about it.

This means keeping our minds pure and staying committed to our wives. Let me speak plainly! Walk away from temptation. Temptation will always knock at your door, but you don't need to open the door and invite it in for a beer. Instead, adore and pursue your wife. After God, she is the most precious thing in your life. If you want an antivirus to temptation, try romance. Gary Chapman wrote a fantastic book called *The Five Love Languages* where you can discover what both you and your wife's love languages are. *The Love Dare* is another great book that will help you to appreciate your marriage and understand your role in it. Start there, and continue

If you want an antivirus to temptation, try romance.

always to pursue your loving wife.

Courageous is a Christian movie that encourages men to embrace the responsibility of fatherhood. In this movie, they have what is called the Resolution, a list of statements that are based upon the highest priorities for men in God's Word. And I really like the idea of it. I encourage you to watch the film! The first statement alone says, "I do solemnly resolve before God to take full responsibility for myself, my wife, and my children. I will love them, protect them, serve them, and teach them the Word of God as the spiritual leader of my home." Now, it goes on to say, "Honor God, be faithful to His church, confront evil, pray for others, practice forgiveness" and so on, and the list as a whole is a big commitment! But when you look at those statements, I don't think most men could say they are even demonstrating two or three of those items in their home, and that is devastating.

When I wasn't serving the Lord for those fifteen years after my dad died, my mom prayed Joshua 24:15 over me, "As for me and my household, we will serve the Lord." She prayed and prayed that her son would step up and lead his family in Christ, but I don't think many men today could demonstrate the resolve my mother displayed.

Husbands today do not have the stones to say, "Come hell or high water, through thick or thin, I am going to hang on for my family, and I am going to lead them for Christ." We just do not have men with that kind of resolve anymore! My observation has been that even those in the "traditional church"—

going back to those 70 million Christians in America—simply grew up in the church, and it was more of a way of life. It became a familiarity, but it was never really tested. This is not to say that God doesn't love them, but if I've learned anything from my time in the military and in running my own business, it's that a man doesn't really know his own manna until he has been pushed to the point of breaking.

I think men need to seek out opportunities in their faith that really pushes themselves. For me, I do not need to go far to look for that. I face struggles every day on all fronts. I'm not going to lie to you, like the Israelites, I complain, but I know that God is putting me under immense pressure to build trust in Him. I fear many husbands are not even pushing themselves or testing themselves to get to a place where they are ready to serve their family, let alone *lead* their family in Christ.

To be fair, men are facing a ton of challenges today that make their role as husband difficult. I think a lot of men have been condemned and beaten down so much that they don't even know how to express themselves anymore. We have become afraid to really say what we think for fear of attack or judgment, so instead, we shrink back from the conflict because we are tired. I think we have gotten to a place in today's society where a man's voice is no longer as important or relevant. Men have become so emasculated that they are despondent and disengaged, therefore forfeiting their roles in society. So how could we possibly expect them to maintain their roles in the home?

Unfortunately, the biggest battle is the one that goes on between our own two ears. Because of the challenges men face, we doubt ourselves and resort to fear and anger. But despite that inner battle, we really have to step up every day and say, "God, do not just give me strength to endure, give me strength to triumph!" God does not just want us to endure. He calls us to victory. He calls us to die for our families if need be.

"God, do not just give me strength to endure, give me strength to triumph!"

Mentality

The glory in this is that we are all capable of being strong husbands. To do so, we must acknowledge our weakness and become deliberate about taking care of our wives and children. The mentality of a strong husband is to trust God, live a life of purpose on purpose, and follow through.

Trust God. Give it all to Him. Lay your burdens down at His feet, and be deliberate and purposeful about it. Cry out to Him! Tell Him you need to be reinforced, saying, "I am fighting for you, man, and I need you." Get yourself to a place in your relationship with God where you believe in yourself to lead your family. You need to be the spiritual leader in your home and set the tone. It's hard for me still! But every night, my wife and I pray before bedtime. We pray with our children, and we pray together, and we ask for forgiveness and protection, and we pray for our enemies. Get on your knees, and lead your family in prayer. And don't worry! He promises to uphold you and strengthen you in His Word. Psalm 89:34 says, "I will not violate my covenant or alter the word that went forth from my lips." He has your back!

Psalm 89:34 says, "I will not violate my covenant or alter the word that went forth from my lips." He has your back!

For me, every day is a battle. There are very few days where there is rest. But whether it's a battle on the work front or a battle being a good husband and father, I still have to wake up energized and ready to go, and so many men do not think they have the energy for that. Trust me, I cannot muster that energy on my own! I need to say every day, "Lord, it's about you, not me. I trust in you, I believe in you, help me muster the energy to prevail!" You can, too.

Live a life of purpose on purpose. Be deliberate about your desire to work for God, and allow God to redirect you when you need it. He has raised you up for a purpose, and it doesn't stop with you just raising and leading your family spiritually. It's about leading others in Christ and having that impact, too. Find your strength to serve your family as the man, and then move that energy out to the rest of the community. Never stop fulfilling your purpose or doubting it. Once He frees you of the chains that bound you, He wants you to help free others of their chains.

Follow through. You must have the attitude of a finisher. You must have such a deep conviction about your obligation as a husband that you want to live it out every day. Are you going to live out the same promise to your wife that God promised you? Hebrews 13:5 says, "I will never leave you nor forsake you." God promised that He's never going to fail you and that He is not going to let you down, and that is absolutely what you need to give to your wife. You have to live it out fully, even when the going is tough—especially when the going is tough.

God promised that He's never going to fail you and that He is not going to let you down, and that is absolutely what you need to give to your wife.

In the heart of every man is a deep desire for justice, and when you are fighting for justice—which is so biblical—it charges your battery! On the contrary, when you do not fight for justice, there's a part of you as a man that dies. Do not give up the fight for your family. Your spouse is looking to you for spiritual guidance. Be there for her in Christ, and be there for your family, always.

Habits

If you talk to any husband, being habitual in your marriage is the largest struggle. It is hard for men to stick to a routine! But we must focus on routinely doing things for our spouse that make them feel loved. We are to love our wives like Christ loved the church (Eph. 5:25).

Every day, my wife is counting on me to be a good husband. She is counting on me to say, "I love you," to pray with her and to cherish her. The relationship you share with your spouse is the most intimate relationship you are ever going to have, so you need accountability! When my wife is weak, she weakens me, and when I am weak, I weaken her, so being mindful about how we take care of ourselves and of one another is holding one another accountable.

We need to regularly, consistently, and habitually be physically present for our wives. When it comes to our bodies, we have an obligation to literally comfort our spouses and to hold them close and be there for them always. I know that when I am present for my wife, that really charges her. But this cannot just be intermittent or whenever it is convenient or easy for us, we need to regularly focus on being present with our spouses and encouraging them in their faith.

Other habits we must develop to be present and engaged husbands include eating right, getting your sleep, exercising, and regularly praying. In the morning, I know I should take time to read my Bible. I know I need quiet time to pray, absorb God's Word, and read content that moves me closer to God and challenges me in my faith. We all struggle with this! It is easy to just watch a show or series on TV and get lost in content that drains us spiritually. In Matthew 26:41 Jesus says, "Watch and pray that you may not enter into temptation. The spirit indeed is willing, but the flesh is weak." Even Jesus knows this is difficult!

We need to regularly focus on being present with our spouses and encouraging them in their faith.

I also know that I need to avoid distractions. Man, I hate distractions! I'm very regimented in my schedule, and my wife and I have gotten very deliberate about not watching the news, not watching TV, and limiting social media, because you can't get that time back. That is the value. A good habit is being deliberate in eliminating things from your life that are a meaningless distraction. If it distracts you from making you a better leader, husband, father or son of God, then you gotta say no to that stuff. I have no idea what's going on in the news today, and I don't care. You might find yourself in conversation and have no idea what people are talking about, and that's embarrassing! But it doesn't matter when you know that God is in control anyway.

Positive habitual behavior strengthens you as a man and strengthens you as a leader in Christ in your home.

Positive habitual behavior strengthens you as a man and strengthens you as a leader in Christ in your home.

Assets

An asset is something we possess. We can either waste it or invest in it to better ourselves. To be a strong and faithful husband, we need to invest in our energy, our time, and our intellect.

Energy. Just like our wives need our physical presence, they need our energy to feel validated, comforted, and loved. You are either going to energize your wife, or you are going to take energy away from her. Some husbands just don't commit the energy, so they are hoarding that asset and, consequently, leaving their wives to do it all themselves. Hence, the over-burdened wife. So many guys bring so little energy to their marriage. It is disheartening, but you can be deliberate and purposeful about the energy you put out in your home, and your wife will feel it. Remember, tune in to her love language.

Time. Yes, I am deliberate about not doing meaningless things, but I'm also deliberate about delegating things that someone else can do for me or saying no to stuff that isn't necessary, so I can spend that time in God's Word with my family and strengthening the faith in our home.

Time is a nonrenewable asset. You can build backup energy and even restore the energy to your wife, but you cannot get time back. If you waste time in a relationship, you lose it, and our society does not recognize how much of a non-recoverable asset time is in our lives. Men especially can so easily lose time doing meaningless, non-purposeful work. How many of us use chores as an excuse not to invest that time in our wives and kids? But when a man is deliberate and conscious about how he spends his time, he is giving his best self to his wife.

Time is a nonrenewable asset.

Intellect versus Wisdom. Twenty years ago, I had intellect, but I was using it for personal affirmation, personal gain, and personal gratification. It was the same intellect I have now, but today my intellect is coupled with experience, and I am choosing to use my intellect in a different way. Intellect is an asset you can deploy for selfish gain or to build up your wife and children and others around you. You can use it to grow in wisdom, which is the real asset.

I am a salesman at heart, and I know how to close a deal. So the question is, What is the deal I am going to close? With the intellect I have now, I know I am going to challenge men to step up as men. You get to choose how you use your intellect, too.

Intellect affords you the ability to constantly amass wisdom and knowledge to better pour into your marriage. Read books together, pray together, immerse yourself in conversation that is going to build from your intellect and draw you closer to one another—in marriage and in faith.

Lead her to Christ. In return, she will be your closest ally in your journey with God.

You can be a beacon of truth in your home. You can guide your wife in faith if you are deliberate about your actions, words, and assets. "Husbands, love your wives, as Christ loved the church and gave himself up for her" (Eph 5:25). Lead her to Christ. In return, she will be your closest ally in your journey with God.

chapter nine:
Fatherhood

Fatherhood

God commands us not to have idols (Exod. 20), but I fear Christians in the church have turned their families into idols, expecting too much of them and falsely worshipping their actions. For example, so many families today are not taking the time to read God's Word, to pray together, or even go to church and engage in ministry because they are too busy running their kids from activity to activity. Somewhere along the way, they chose to exhaust their assets—their time and energy—into meaningless activity that runs their marriage into the ground and alienates God from the home.

Because parents have become so consumed with the "need" for their kids to excel, they have fallen prey to idolizing their kids' future and living vicariously through them to the point that core values are completely being missed. There is not even discussion in the home of what a family's values are, and that is far more relevant in life than winning the next big game! Parents are no longer clear on their "Why" in life, so neither are their kids. And if your "Why" is because the "Joneses" are doing it, is that really a good enough reason?

We have little girls in our society who are amazing figure skaters but have no sense of well-being, of belonging or purpose. We've got NHL hockey players who are stronger, faster, and more skilled than the guys who played for the love of the game in the '50s, '60s, and '70s but have little to no character development as young men. And the burden of that responsibility rests on us, the parents, the ones who have turned the rearing of their children into the rearing of superstars and celebrities instead of men and women of noble character. It's not that we don't want our children to do well in life, but let's be clear on what our definition of success really is. If success in your home is achieving great heights by society's standards but not having God at the center, then we've really missed the mark, and I think we can do better.

Parents are no longer clear on their "Why" in life, so neither are their kids.

I say to my kids all the time, "I am so proud of you. I want to see you succeed. You are destined for great things!" And it is important to empower them. But then, I continue on, "As your father, there is nothing more important to me than you knowing who Christ is and that you trust Him for your life. Let God be your guide." They can still be great figure skaters, but imagine the change if they are grounded in *who* gave them that ability and responsibility.

It is important that we use those words when we empower our kids. Because as soon as we stop including God in conversation with them, we are setting them up for a life of spiritual fatherlessness that we in no uncertain terms know by now is not a good way of life. *We owe this to our children.*

So many fathers in society have lost what really matters when it comes to raising their families, but I am not going to let society dictate to me how I should be raising my children. More than ever before, parents have this terrible need to be accepted and to fit into a community to the point where they lose sight of their values and instead do anything to appease the "audience"—a society we could never live up to.

We are very deliberate about engaging our children in ministry, involving them in as much as we can and letting them know what is most important to us as a family. If parents choose not to be deliberate about this, their kids will be raised by a delinquent society. There is a cultural insurgence into our homes that must be thwarted, and that begins by being deliberate about how we raise our children.

This conversation is unique to our times. Because of their access to technology, our children are growing up way too fast, but they are still just children! We have eleven-year-olds who have entire worlds at their fingertips. We have devices that are more powerful than the first computer that put a man on the moon, and we are putting them in a six-year-old's lap. We are letting iPads entertain four-year-olds while we work around the house or eat our dinners. And, worst of all, we as the adults in the home are not being deliberate enough about putting down *our own* devices, therefore, acting as zombie parents in front of the family and letting our kids think that is OK. This is a disgrace. Technology should be making our lives better! It should be revered as a dangerous tool, but aren't we just taking advantage of it?

When it comes to our spouses, we need to intentionally give them our time and energy. But when it comes to our children, not only do we need to give them our time and energy, we need to be teaching them, too, how to buffer their own time, energy, and resources. We teach by what we do, and our actions are incredibly powerful.

We teach by what we do, and our actions are incredibly powerful.

Whether you are a working dad, a stay-at-home-dad or a single parent, we need to stay engaged in our children's lives and be proactive however we can, as much as we can. Our love for them matters most of all.

Mentality and Habits

Do you love your children enough to sacrifice your own life for them? Would you die for them? Of course you would, but men today have to fight a different fight. We naturally want to protect our families, and we do, but now we also have to fight against technology, cultural society, legal systems, a demanding school system and media. And, meanwhile, all those structures have positioned dads as absentee, non-interested and complacent. To defeat this, we need to develop a mentality that is stronger than the impossible society that is trying to bring us down, and we need to do that on our knees and in prayer.

The first belief to develop is a sacrificial attitude *for God*. God is my Father in Heaven. His Son died for me because He loved me enough to put His life on the cross for me. Now, it is my responsibility to my family to lay down my life for them, but only out of love for God and out of obedience to Him. It sounds very noble to say that a man would lay his life down for his wife and kids, but if you do not include God in that, then that man is really just a glorified bodyguard. You are to be more than a bodyguard. As a father, your role is to protect, preserve, and defend your children's minds, bodies, and souls in Christ. And don't be fearful in this! God loves our children more than we do, and if we ask Him to help us fight the Goliaths, He will. "Before I formed you in the womb I knew you," he says in Jeremiah 1:5.

What worries me is when a man says that he loves his kids so much that he is going to compromise God's will for his family just to please them. When a man backs down on what he knows is godly prescribed wisdom, he is taking God out of the home. That man is usurping God on account of his own weakness.

When a man backs down on what he knows is godly prescribed wisdom, he is taking God out of the home.

For example, if I have a wayward daughter, I can most assuredly tell you that I will have the courage to remind her of her obligation as a woman before God. Of course, I'm still going to be her father and love her, but the key is to not let my love for her blind me of my responsibility to lead her in Christ. So many men say they love their children so much, they will support them in acts that they know are wrong or disrespectful to others or God's design for their life, just so the child doesn't feel bad. But as fathers, we cannot back down. Our mentality must be first a sacrificial attitude for God and then to remind our children of our responsibilities to Him. They may reject you for a season, but if that wisdom is delivered with love and followed through with patience and grace, then you have done your job as a parent.

We've got to be a shepherd to our families. I believe we need to disciple them, too, but a shepherd is willing to go to great lengths to keep that sheep *in* the fold, whereas discipling them is when the sheep is already in the fold and you are nurturing it. If a child goes astray, you would go get her, like any loving father. You would counsel her and bring her back, but then you would not be afraid to discipline her. If she is in the fold and growing, you would love her, encourage her, and keep pouring into her. Both roles matter. Proverbs 3:11-12 says, "My son, do not despise the Lord's discipline or be weary of his reproof, for the Lord reproves him whom he loves, as a father the son in whom he delights."

I believe we shepherd and disciple our children by praying blessings over them. As a dad, I have a charge to pray a blessing over my kids and pray that the decision they make to trust God for their lives will continue in them as they age. And I need to encourage that of them, too. They are battling the societal pull to reject God, so I need to always be encouraging faith in God in their lives. It's a consistent, habitual blessing on their life.

If I can see that my daughter is upset about something, I will ask her, "Do you want me to pray with you?" She'll most often say yes, so then I'll get on my knees next to her, hold her hand and I'll pray that the Holy Spirit will just be with my daughter and comfort her. This matters to her! And the Holy Spirit is the "Great Comforter."

Surely, we pray as a family unit, too, but it's important to pray individually with your children. When we pray as a family, we pray about challenges we are facing or we pray for others—it's a lot of outward focus, a way to be vulnerable and authentic with the kids. I think it is important to be transparent with your children and allow them to be part of the process, whatever that may be!

But then, when we pray alone with them, it becomes solely about the child and about where they are with God and whatever struggles they are facing. I think there is really a need to say with your child, "There is a Father in Heaven who loves you and adores you, and He has given you an earthly father who is flawed." I say this to my daughters all the time! But I remind them, too, that their father's job is to be the best demonstration of *Him*, God the Father in Heaven. Proverbs 20:7 says, "The righteous who walks in his integrity—blessed are his children after him!" I help them to realize that I have this job. And even though I am not perfect at it, God *is* perfect, and when I pray blessings over them, I speak with authority, and I reiterate that. God will not fail you.

Along with praying together, I think another critical habit is to read the Bible together as a family. Sit down and read small excerpts together, and then talk about it. When we do this in our home, I can see the kids really engaged, and the Bible seems to have even more relevance to them when it is all of us doing it together. I see them thinking, If Dad is taking the time to engage, then I want to understand. We also watch movies, sermons, or documentaries that teach God's Word. When they were younger, the girls loved *Buck Denver Asks: What's in the Bible?* I admit, we loved it, too!

Talk to your kids often, and talk openly about God. Our kids are absolutely a part of our decision-making processes, and they are aware that a part of that process is to leave it before God and pray about it, to literally say, "Lord, we leave this with you." Our kids are not fearful because we do not tip-toe around life for the sake of their innocence. Instead, we talk about everything and empower them to step up and honor God in their daily life. My kids don't even get out of the car to go to school in the morning without me praying over them. We talk about God in everything we do.

Assets

In our home, we have what we call a "war room." It is an intimate corner of our home where we pray together. I think one of the most important assets to fatherhood is to reserve a place in your home that serves only the purpose of meeting God and pouring out your hearts to Him together. In this place, we set out all your Christian content. We write our prayers on sticky notes on the wall and verses from the Bible that strengthen our faith. Regardless of how you treat this place, it is comfortable, inviting, and it is an asset to keeping God in your home.

Another asset in fatherhood is to eat dinner together as a family. My dad was a busy man, but at 5:30 every night, we gathered at the kitchen table, and we ate as a family. I'm really proud of the fact that for my family today, we meet at the kitchen table, we hold hands and say grace, we thank God for our food, and we welcome Him in. It really becomes the first time in the evening where God is invited into our presence, and then that continues on for the remainder of the night.

If we aren't at the kitchen table eating and praying, we sit and play board games together as a family, delighting and investing our time in one another.

I want to say that we do leverage technology in our home as an asset, but it's counter-cultural and actually used to build up our family. We put in Christian DVDs or music in the background, and when we are driving in the car with the kids, we like to sing certain songs together from artists who encourage us in our faith. One of our favourite groups is Mercy Me.

There is no better way to point to our Creator than to take in His creation with your kids.

Lastly, as a man, it is important to spend time outdoors as a family and to let nature be an asset to raising your children. Play together outside! God created this earth for us, and my kids get that. There is no better way to point to our Creator than to take in His creation with your kids.

"And the Holy Spirit descended on him in bodily form, like a dove; and a voice came from heaven,

'You are my beloved Son; with you I am well pleased' " (Luke 3:22). Be an intentional parent. Even though you endure the scars of fatherlessness, do not let your own children suffer the same fate. Let them know they are loved, and guide them to a life with Christ.

chapter ten:

Finish Strong

Finish Strong

I believe every man has a deep, unstoppable desire in his heart to finish. I believe we long for a sense of completion, to be able to look back and see our labor come to fruition and have that closure. Only then can our hearts proclaim, "Look what I did. Look what I have accomplished. Look what I have built." We want this for our lives, and I want this for you here.

Men are finishers. If they do not live out their authentic self and do not deliver, a part of them will die. It is a God-given mandate to step up as a man and follow through. Have you come this far, in this book and on your broken road, not to follow through?

Now is your time to finish.

God finishes what He starts. Even though we often don't know how to finish, God will show you the way, because He always finishes what He starts, and He will not abandon you. Finishing is written on your heart. Philippians 1:6 says, "He who began a good work in you will bring it to completion at the day of

Christ Jesus."

I believe men desire to be finishers because we like to work. We like to feel tired. We like to have purpose and to leave it all out there for the day. We love to finish because that brings us satisfaction, and we like to feel satisfied. When men complete a task, there is well-deserved dignity. God hates pride (Prov. 16:5), but he does want us to humbly feel accomplished, because it makes a man feel whole.

When I finish something, I feel like I can take on two more things twice as hard. I've tested my limits, I know I can do it, and now I want to try something more. Last year, I ran a half-marathon, and this year, I'm going to run a full marathon, because I now know I can. Being a strong finisher produces even more ambition. If you have rebuilt your broken road here and have established a relationship with God, imagine how your next chapter will go! Finishing empowers us to achieve even more than we ever thought possible. What an incredible reward, to be able to see our work through.

When I was in the military, we had to complete some navigational training in which they would dump you 20 kilometers out in the middle of nowhere in the middle of the night with only a map, a flashlight, and a compass, and you had to find your way to the finish by daylight. When I had to complete this, I was coming down with something that morning and, by that night, I was sick. It was also pouring rain and a cold summer night.

I began, and as soon as they dumped me, I was

able to get my bearings right away by orientating myself and triangulating my position from a nearby collapsed church. But about 2 km in, I fell down a ravine. It was rainy and wet and pitch black dark, and I lost my footing and fell to the bottom. I was hurt and sick, and now I had lost my map, too. I was able to find my compass and flashlight, so I climbed up the other side of the ravine, calmed my nerves, reviewed the map in my mind and then literally drew it out from memory onto my log book. From there, I barely made each checkpoint and had to wade through a swamp that was up to my armpits because I knew I wouldn't finish in time otherwise, but I did it.

I finished. What I took away from that experience was this deep sense of accomplishment, because I was faced with tons of obstacles. Both internally and externally, there were things that were in my lotus of control and outside my lotus of control, and my determination came from not wanting to let those circumstances get the better of me and to finish strong instead. That was over twenty years ago, but I can still feel that deliberate desire within my body to finish that task, and I urge you to feel that sense now. I urge you to not give up.

I see men giving up so easily. The hard part about being a successful husband, father, and man is that there is no quick gratification. And when the road is broken, it seems gratifying to just give up and not try, as opposed to doubling down and staying engaged. And only then is there true reward.

When we follow through, our wives can count on

The hard part about being a successful husband, father, and man is that there is no quick gratification.

us and our families feel secure. It would be devastating for our children to watch us give up and for them to then experience their own fatherlessness. Finishing is the difference between success and failure. There is no gray area. Either you finish this, or you don't.

How to be a Finisher

Go to your mentor. Hebrews 12:1 says, "Therefore, since we are surrounded by so great a cloud of witnesses, let us also lay aside every weight, and sin which clings so closely, and let us run with endurance the race that is set before us." You need accountability through men who remind you of your obligation to not give up and finish the task.

Declare to your mentor and to your peer groups what you are going to do. Name it and claim it, and say it to enough people that you won't want to let them down. Confide in them, ask them to pray for you, and allow them to encourage you and push you and come beside you with a rallying cry as you work. Allow yourself to see that people are rooting for you!

I am rooting for you.

What are your values in life? If your current state is in conflict with those values, then how are you going to get aligned? For example, if you pride yourself on aspiring to excellence, then are you acting excellently as a husband, dad, and leader? If you value kindness, are you demonstrating that both in the home and in public? If there is any conflict with what you value and what your actual actions are, then you will never find the peace you are seeking here. Values matter in this, they are indeed an asset to help you finish strong. Peace will perpetually elude you if you live out of alignment with your values.

Peace will perpetually elude you if you live out of alignment with your values.

Familiarize yourself with your habits and your assets, and be clear on how you are going to follow through on each of them each day. If I have learned anything in life, it's that it takes at least twenty-one days in a row to create a habit, and you cannot develop multiple habits at once. So deploy your assets, and be deliberate about establishing one habit at a time, then moving onto the next. Do not get bottle-necked here. Work intentionally and patiently with yourself and with resolution.

And finish with Him in mind. Get on your knees, be a humble praying man, embrace the gospel, and embrace Him. Only then can you succeed.

Teddy Roosevelt once said, "It is not the critic who counts; not the man who points out how the strong man stumbles, or where the doer of deeds could have done them better. The credit belongs to the man who is actually in the arena, whose face is marred by dust and sweat and blood; who strives valiantly; who errs, who comes short again and again, because there is no effort without error and shortcoming; but who does actually strive to do the deeds; who knows great enthusiasms, the great devotions; who spends himself in a worthy cause; who at the best knows in the end the triumph of high achievement, and who at the worst, if he fails, at least fails while daring greatly, so that his place shall never be with those cold and timid souls who neither know victory nor defeat." Your strife is worth it. I implore you to triumph.

Do not ask yourself what you are going to start as a result of this book. Ask yourself what you will finish.

My heart's desire for you is to have an action plan and to finish it. Do not ask yourself what you are going to start as a result of this book. Ask yourself what you will finish.

CONCLUSION

My dad was a decisive man, and he always followed through. I lost him as my guide and mentor and leader in life when I was fifteen years old, but today, I am not fatherless because I have my Father in heaven to lead me, to forgive me, and to guide me constantly toward my purpose in life. Just like my earthly father always did, I will follow through in my actions, because I have God to get me there.

Men love to be tested. We are thrilled at the opportunity to explore and take action. One way to take action here is to step out. I encourage you to step out of your comfort zone and start being the man you want to be for your wives, your children, your friends, and community. If you want to be the man, then be the man! Join organizations that matter, volunteer where it will make a difference, and seek purpose. I wrote this book because I want to help other men—men like me who once felt lost and without purpose. Because purpose will give you hope, and hope changes everything.

Luke 11:9 says, "Ask, seek, and knock." As you take risks and finish what you started, God promises to be there. You just have to say yes to Him. There will be setbacks. There will be disappointments. But God will see your heart and your efforts, and He will direct you toward a framework that is healthy, wholesome, and pleasing to you and Him. Do not let your fatherlessness overtake you, and do not be discouraged. The time to live in Christ is now.

ABOUT THE AUTHOR

Jonathan Lewis is the president of Eastport Financial Group Inc. and author of 'Deep Water' a book on facing the giant of fatherlessness for men. He is the dedicated husband to Sara Lewis and father of two beautiful daughters. Jonathan lives in Hebbville, NS. Faith, family, community, philanthropy and last but not least, entrepreneurship, are all deeply entrenched cornerstones that have guided him for many years. Jonathan and Sara are invested at any given time in upwards of 2 or 3 startups including most recently SEL of the Earth. SEL is Sara's most recent "baby" in the fashion space. Jonathan has been personally involved with numerous charities and community-based pursuits locally, nationally and internationally; striving to change peoples lives through volunteering, fundraising and advocating. As an accomplished public speaker, Jonathan has never tired of delivering a message of compassion while challenging other entrepreneurs and business owners to think beyond themselves. Whether in his personal life or professional life he has never been one to settle for mediocrity.

"I am told I bring a dynamic and unique energy to every situation as I challenge and push others to aspire to work towards and be something so much bigger than they themselves thought possible. I believe all of us have God given talents waiting to be unleashed."

"In life I think all of us ask, at some point...WHY am I here? What is my purpose? Often this is when we are facing insurmountable odds and feel overwhelmed by what life is throwing at us. I know I was there as a young man. I encourage you to take the time to discover your "WHY". Mine is to help at-risk youth. It is to help the fatherless. It is to fight for justice for those that can't and let them know they aren't alone. I believe HOPE heals hearts!"